D1550896

Town&Country

The Guide to Intelligent Giving

• • •

Make a Difference in the World—and in Your Own Life

Joanna L. Krotz

HEARST BOOKS
A division of Sterling Publishing Co., Inc.

New York / London
www.sterlingpublishing.com

Copyright © 2009 by Joanna L. Krotz

Library of Congress Cataloging-in-Publication Data

Krotz, Joanna L.
  Town & country : a guide to intelligent giving : how you can make a
difference in the world / Joanna Krotz.
    p. cm.
  Includes index.
  ISBN 978-1-58816-761-3 (alk. paper)
  1. Charities. 2. Generosity. I. Title. II. Title: Town and country.
  HV40.K74 2009
  361.7'4--dc22
                                                    2008051742

10 9 8 7 6 5 4 3 2 1

Published by Hearst Books
A division of Sterling Publishing Co., Inc.
387 Park Avenue South, New York, NY 10016

Town & Country and Hearst Books are trademarks of
Hearst Communications, Inc.

www.townandcountrymag.com

For information about custom editions, special sales, premium and
corporate purchases, please contact Sterling Special Sales Department
at 800-805-5489 or specialsales@sterlingpublishing.com.

Distributed in Canada by Sterling Publishing
c/o Canadian Manda Group, 165 Dufferin Street
Toronto, Ontario, Canada M6K 3H6

Distributed in Australia by Capricorn Link (Australia) Pty. Ltd.
P.O. Box 704, Windsor, NSW 2756 Australia

Printed in USA

Interior design by Chris Welch

Sterling ISBN: 978-1-58816-761-3

CONTENTS

FOREWORD

No other nation in the world is as generous as the United States of America. That's a fact. If it's not part of our DNA, then it is a part of our history and is something to be proud of. Think back to early philanthropists such as J.P. Morgan, Andrew Carnegie, Henry Clay Frick, John Jacob Astor, Andrew Mellon, and John D. Rockefeller. They funded hospitals, schools, concert halls, museums, and other institutions bearing their names, and in doing so helped to advance progress in medicine, science, education, and culture. In a capitalist society, the government will only do so much. It is often up to the private sector to support programs for education and the performing arts, to push forward research and to help those who cannot help themselves.

In recent years, charitable giving has become more

diverse and creative. Consider the late Paul Newman. As an accomplished actor, he could have rested on his laurels and lived a pleasant life in Connecticut with his wife, Joanne Woodward, and his children. Instead, he began whipping up batches of his recipe for salad dressing, bottling it, selling it under the name Newman's Own, and then donating the proceeds to charity. Salad dressing led to popcorn, salsa, and other products, and a philanthropic empire was born. At the time of his death in 2008, his enterprise (which lives on) had raised more than $250 million and enabled him to open his Hole-in-the-Wall Camps for kids with cancer and other life-threatening illnesses.

A whole new generation of philanthropists has followed in Paul Newman's footsteps, coming up with inventive ways to approach giving and establish foundations for important causes. Consider Bill and Melinda Gates, Warren Buffet, and Oprah Winfrey, whose efforts are wide-ranging in their scope and global in their reach. But you needn't be a billionaire to be philanthropic—or even a grownup. Kids can learn to be charitable at an early age and can experience the rewards of volunteering. Young men and women can sign up for mentoring programs and lend their talents and energies to countless endeavors that involve public service. As adults, individuals can become active change agents for causes that are meaningful to them.

There are all sorts of reasons that people today give their money and their time. When natural disasters—such as the tsunami in Southeast Asia and Hurricane Katrina in the American South—occur, the world leaps to its feet to help.

When tragedy strikes close to home (a disabled child, an elderly relative diagnosed with Alzheimer's, a stroke or cancer victim) families and sometimes entire communities rise to the occasion in magnanimous ways. In the end, that is the best kind of giving: that which comes from both the head and the heart.

How to be charitable, to whom or what and in what form is the premise of *The Guide to Intelligent Giving*. Its author, Joanna Krotz, has contributed many articles to *Town & Country* and has a full understanding of the subject. The book is based on her own vast knowledge as well as interviews with informed individuals, many of whom started their own foundations and have a great deal of wisdom to impart. The lessons that these donors learned are worth reading about, and their advice is priceless. There are many clichés about philanthropy: "Charity begins at home" and "It is better to give than to receive" are two of them. But as with any cliché, there is more than a grain of truth to the message. We hope you will find some guidance in this book and, moreover, that it will lead you to a fuller, more gratifying life.

Pamela Fiori
Editor in Chief
Town & Country

Chapter 1

CAN YOU REALLY MAKE A DIFFERENCE?

HOW WE GIVE TODAY

Wherever you go, whomever you talk to, the path of today's philanthropy invariably starts with someone's story—a moment when overwhelming need meets an outstretched hand. Such one-to-one connections ignite the dry kindling of obligation into the emotional flame of personal engagement. And that heat tends to build, too, gaining intensity and commitment the longer you remain involved.

For example, when investment banker Jewelle Bickford traveled to Rwanda a few years ago and saw firsthand the aftershocks of ethnic genocide, she returned to New York with altered priorities. "It changes your life," says Bickford. Soon, all of her charitable efforts were focused on helping survivors of war. Similarly, when Jeffrey Swartz, chief executive of Timberland, the international apparel company, helped paint some walls one afternoon in a New Hampshire group home for recovering young drug addicts, he came "face-to-face with the headlines you read in the newspaper," and was also utterly changed. Before long, Swartz created a company program that's become a model for corporate giving nationwide. And when a young Los Angeles pediatrician named Astrid Heger volunteered at a local hospital, she discovered that sexually abused children suffered repeated and ongoing trauma because of legally required examinations. Heger launched a one-woman campaign to reverse such practices that ultimately set new and compassionate legal precedents in every state in the country.

Welcome to the power of one.

Philanthropy Has Become Democratic, Diverse, and Dynamic

The pages that follow reveal a host of similar sparks, offering tales of personal awakening and moments of passion that turn to purposeful action—all of them designed to inspire and enlighten you. Philanthropy has been changing with the times. Abuzz with new energy and options, philanthropy is being shaped by a range of accelerating trends, including the nonstop speed of information technology, the blurring of for-profit and nonprofit giving—which is redefining the nature of charities—and the heightened scrutiny of nonprofits from media and government. It is being transformed by a world grown so intimate that trouble across the globe hits our screen as if it were around the corner. Community is now worldwide, and global need, palpable. Witness the broadening international consensus to take on the challenge of climate change. Consider the unprecedented and spontaneous resources that rose to relieve the pain of the Asian tsunami, Hurricane Katrina, or the earthquake in China.

Of late, many more Americans of every age, income, and color are choosing to give, a reflection, no doubt, of our shrinking world. But that newfound generosity also flows from the rise of unparalleled affluence over the past two decades. Perhaps above all, philanthropy has been evolving because of this new and younger wealth. For the first time in American history, thousands of individuals and families have more money than their kids will need. Much of it is first generation, as well. That is, earned wealth.

Evidence of the rising tide in American giving is unmistakable, even in the face of tougher economic realities. In 2007, as the nation's housing market sank and oil and gas prices soared, individual Americans still accounted for 75 percent of the record-setting $306 billion in annual charitable donations, according to Giving USA Foundation, a charitable research group. The United States alone accounted for slightly more than half of all global online giving in 2007, or $10.4 billion of the total $20 billion, according to the Harvard University Initiative on Social Enterprise.

Women, too, with their increased earning power, professional skills, and control over their financial lives, are reconfiguring the face of philanthropy. The latest IRS reports about giving by gender show that gifts from women topped those from men by nearly $5 billion in 2005, or $22 billion compared to $17 billion. That's a significant shift from the last IRS gender analysis in 1997, when men gave nearly 18 billion and women gave just under 15 billion.

Overall, about nine out of every ten American households now give to charitable causes. Donor-activist Barbara Dobkin sums up this impulse very simply: "When you look at the world today and you have money to spend, how can you not take part in philanthropy?" In 2006, Dobkin contributed $6 million of the fortune created by her investment banker husband, Eric, to fund the safety and survival of women, including a million-dollar-plus contribution to Women Moving Millions, a fund-raising campaign for women's causes that is on track to raise $150 million.

Donors Are Different, Too

As a result of these converging forces, a new breed of donor is emerging. People who give are no longer so content to hand over money to faceless catchall causes. Instead, the new donors are engaged and hands-on, focused on making a specific impact today rather than on leaving a legacy for a future they won't see. "The interesting thing about philanthropy now is that the people driving it are not dead," says economist and fund-raising consultant Susan Raymond at

Changing Our World, drawing a contrast with past traditions, when philanthropic dollars largely flowed from estates and bequests. "And because they're not dead," she continues, "we can focus on accomplishments rather than just the money. It's a sobering experience for philanthropy." That focus is likely to intensify even if the flow of charitable dollars slows a bit as the economy cools. Sector researchers point out that in the past forty years, real declines in the country's individual giving never lasted longer than a year, except after the 9/11 attacks and the oil embargo crisis of the mid-1970s.

Unsurprisingly, then, the new (and alive) donors are experimenting with new (and energetic) kinds of philanthropic impact, such as forming egalitarian giving circles that make collective decisions about their gifts. Individuals are setting up donor-advised funds with community foundations and other financial hosts in order to retain a voice in grant making. They are establishing innovations in family philanthropy. The nation's nearly 36,000 family foundations gave a whopping $16 billion in 2006, an increase of 13 percent from the previous year, according to the latest report from the Foundation Center, a national research group based in New York. What's more, nearly seven out of every ten (67 percent) of those family foundations were established since 1990. Sisters and cousins, fathers and nephews, moms and grandfathers are getting together to ask the tough questions, review proposals, make site visits, and manage operations and finances. Roughly half (48 percent) of all family foundations grant less than $50,000 annually.

The Change in Defining Success

Taken together, today's forward-looking activists, with greater or lesser resources, are fueling the growing power of strategic philanthropy. They are making individual choices about where and when to engage, about what causes matter to them, and about what methods are most effective in making a difference. "Acts of kindness can be done in a day," says Colleen Willoughby, founder of the pioneering Washington Women's Foundation, in Seattle. "Community building is the work of a lifetime."

This shift is provoking a significant reexamination of how to measure philanthropic success. The new mantra demands accountability, transparency, and sometimes, performance metrics—or so-called impact philanthropy. Donors want to track where their assets go. They want to leverage more than money. They want to harness their skills and access to power in order to influence policy, politicians, corporations, and neighbors. Volunteers want to know that organizational resources are truly utilized to advance the mission. "Many of today's really big fortunes have been made in finance and in technology, arenas that lend themselves to quantifiable measures of success," says Katherine Fulton, president of the Monitor Institute, a philanthropy research group. "Many new donors coming in therefore want measurable results, things they can count."

Amid these changes, the interest in giving has increasingly turned to addressing social inequities. Donors are focusing on systemic change for social ills, both at home and worldwide. For instance, "Are you truly helping the homeless by building more shelters?" asks H. Peter Karoff, founder of the Philanthropic Initiative, a Boston-based consultancy. "Wouldn't we be better off working on issues of education, job training, and child care in order to combat homelessness?" For emphasis, he points to a huge $10 million food bank recently built in Atlanta. "What does such a facility say about what we will need fifty years from now?" Should we be spending time, dollars, and energy on creating bigger and bigger shelters to warehouse more and more homeless? Or should we put the money and resources to work creating jobs and skills that could eradicate the reasons people become homeless? At its best, this orientation turns philanthropy into a strategic tool, making it bolder, more flexible, and keenly far-reaching. It sets out to win the war instead of fighting yet another battle. As Geoffrey Canada, CEO of the Harlem Children's Zone, puts it, "I don't want to feed a hungry child. I want to stamp out hunger."

Always, though, such benchmarking is driven by passion, by the reason activists and donors get involved in the first place: to make a difference.

What's in It for You?

In this guide, you'll find up-to-date, easy-to-use news and tools about becoming involved in philanthropy and about practical ways to make an impact today, tomorrow, and next year. No question—if givers spend time learning how to be

Who Will Be Giving in the Future?
Ten Emerging Donor Trends

1. Racial and ethnic diversity among donors will increase across the country.

2. Wealth appreciation will become significant among virtually all donor communities, including African American, Asian, Hispanic, gay, women, youth, and self-made ones.

3. Interest in international giving will increase among all types of donors.

4. "Flash giving"—triggered by international conflicts, famine, and natural disasters and highlighted by the media—has the potential to engage and empower many donors. It is likely to become the entry point or primary mode of giving for many donors.

5. Foreign-born U.S. residents in all income categories will significantly increase the money they send home.

6. Increasingly, donors will be attracted to self-education and peer giving communities or gatherings that maintain connections and sponsor events.

7. More and more donors will manage all of their giving—both flash and more sustained—via specialized Internet portals.

8. Giving by faith-based donors, currently responsible for the majority of the country's charitable gifts, will turn more complex as religious groups become polarized and politicized.

9. Donor demand for streamlined 24/7 online interfaces will push for change in the business and operational sides of nonprofits and community foundations.

more effective, we all will get a decidedly bigger bang for our collective charitable buck.

You'll also find carefully considered advice and smart methods for identifying the right cause for you, tapping advisors, evaluating financial options, measuring success or impact, leveraging tax strategies, and much more. Each chapter is meant to offer help in a different arena. So if you're already immersed in a mission, feel free to jump to Chapter 9 to learn about ramping up to the next level. Or skip to Chapter 10 to find out how best to engage the next generation.

Despite the wide lens on trends and changes and the focus on a full range of charitable issues and details, at its core, this guide is designed to move you into the path of philanthropy and to motivate you to stretch out your hand. Once you do, it's an odds-on bet that you will find nothing else as rewarding or life affirming.

You'll also be joining some very good company.

Chapter 2

WHAT MAKES A GOOD GIVER?

TAKING THE FIRST STEPS

As philanthropy and the nonprofit sector adjust to a new world of need and increasing social activism, philanthropists are no longer defined by deep pockets. Rather, you become one by examining your values and finding the cause that moves you enough to dedicate money, time, and skills to it.

JOIN THE
CONVERSATION

"I don't think philanthropy can be considered just for people with significant wealth. It cuts across class and status. It's about civic participation."
—CAMERON JORDAN,
THIRD-GENERATION
PHILANTHROPIST

"When I talk to my kids about philanthropy, I try to talk around the issues of both generosity and values," says philanthropist Abby Disney, grandniece of Walt Disney and granddaughter of the media company's cofounder, Roy Disney. A longtime advocate for women's rights, Disney funds programs via the Daphne Foundation, a family foundation she established in 1991 to battle poverty in New York City. "To make the decision about what to contribute to," she continues, "I ask my kids to think about what really pisses them off, to think about giving to the things you get a little mad about."

The individual moment that triggers long-term commitment can be just that direct. Somewhere along the way, you decide to step forward, whether to soothe the pain of people in need, to work toward righting wrongs that make you indignant, to build an organization you deem worthy, or to help fulfill a mission that presses your buttons. Certainly, homework and planning must kick in later, when you're figuring out how much to give and choosing among the many ways to give—and those options are fully explored in later chapters. But for starters, the impulse to engage, the desire to give, comes simply from the head and the heart, not from any bank account. Think that's merely a timeworn platitude? Then you haven't heard about Oseola McCarty.

Philanthropy Does Not Have to Start with Money

In 1995, at the age of eighty-seven, McCarty, a laundress in Hattiesburg, Mississippi, donated $150,000—the bulk of her life savings—to a scholarship fund for black students at the University of Southern Mississippi. "I sure wanted to set up an example," she said at the time. Within a few years, McCarty's gift had doubled, because she motivated so many additional gifts from others. This unusual woman, who was forced to drop out of school at age eight to begin working, soon turned into a celebrity. She was feted by the media, profiled in features and interviews, and was even the honored guest of then president Clinton at a dinner of the Congressional Black Caucus in Washington, D.C. McCarty died in 1999. Her legacy, the Oseola McCarty Scholarship Fund, is going strong.

Besides inspiration, McCarty's example provides a few practical lessons. Goodness knows how many nickels and dollars she accumulated bit by bit over how many years to build that $150,000 fund. But she waited to make her donation until the gift would make the utmost impact. For sure, charitable impulses always are admirable. But being able to see and hear and point to a substantial difference? That's truly inspiring. McCarty also turned out to be a strategic planner, investing in education for young people who otherwise would not have had the opportunity. Her gift had a ripple effect across time and lives. McCarty's extraordinary generosity added up to a lot more than the media story du jour (though media attention is hardly a bad thing, as it often helps up the ante on giving). Her scholarship fund continues to further the cause she embraced to this day. And it will keep funding students tomorrow.

So that's the key. Not just to give, but to give with impact—and heart.

Ten Fast-Track Ideas for Charitable Giving

If you're eager to get started, here are some suggestions to get going right away. As you read these, you'll probably think of a dozen more.

1. Work alongside your teenager in a community service project. Call the local community center or YMCA to ask where best to put your efforts.

2. Give a blanket, food, or clothing to the homeless person you see every morning.

3. Volunteer to help clean up a local park or playground.

4. Offer to babysit for neighbors who can rarely afford a night out.

5. Shop for groceries or run errands for a shut-in or a senior.

6. Volunteer to help with reading or other mentoring programs. Call the local school or community college to find out how.

7. Donate a talent or skill—whether bookkeeping or graphic design—to an organization that works for a cause you believe in.

8. Spend a day working at the local ASPCA or animal shelter.

9. Give your frequent-flier miles or club points to a charity or to the Make a Wish Foundation.

10. Buy equipment for and/or offer to coach the local soccer or Little League team.

Remember: Donating money, becoming engaged in philanthropy, volunteering your time, or extending an act of kindness doesn't require a huge investment or elaborate planning. Just decide to get involved and jump in.

Effective Philanthropy Is
Something You Learn

People aren't born knowing how to give in a transformative way. Effective philanthropy is something you learn. It takes planning and attention, steps and missteps, to effect real change. "Charity is reactive," explains the Washington Women's Foundation's Colleen Willoughby. "You see an immediate need and you respond, almost without thinking. Philanthropy is intentional and usually extends over a longer period of time."

To begin, you want to identify a cause that will drive your pocketbook and interest over time. Try to carve out goals you can actually accomplish, building relationships with a host of varied partners, stakeholders, and grantees. And stay focused, concentrating on outcomes and the mission you choose.

You must also have passion. "The most important thing is to give money to the things you care about," says multimillionaire entrepreneur and philanthropist Lewis Cullman, who, along with his wife, Dorothy, has so far given away about $250 million, leveraging this sum through challenge and matching grants to raise millions more. Focusing mainly on science, education, and cultural charities in New York City, Cullman usually earmarks major gifts for specific projects. For instance, a few years back he gave $10 million to the New York City Public Library to establish a center for writers and scholars, with an additional $5 million pledged in a bequest. "I fund programs instead of buildings," he says. This, he believes, lets him track results more effectively. "But I will fund a building if it's needed to house a specific program." One example is the recently completed Lewis B. and Dorothy Cullman Education and Research Building at the Museum of Modern Art in New York.

The critical part of deciding how to engage is to carefully consider whether the investment you've chosen can actually move the needle. Will your involvement make the difference you're seeking? If so, is that difference enough to make you feel the investment will be worthwhile over the long term?

These are tough questions. And only you have the right answers. As Madelyn Ringgold, senior philanthropic advisor at JPMorgan Chase, says, "Philanthropy is as individual and deeply personal as the person doing the giving. There are no real rules, like there are for being a good investor. We don't have metrics for being a good giver." What is clear is that

Four Steps to Impact

There are four basic questions to answer before you can begin to give effectively:

1. What constituency or group do you want to nurture?

2. How much will you contribute annually? What amount is comfortable?

3. What is your goal or what will you fund?

4. Most important, how will you define success?

when you can point to tangible results, you'll feel a great sense of achievement and purpose. That's what makes the learning process so rewarding and why it's smart to set goals you can actually accomplish.

Gary Sinise Figured Out How to Make His Gifts Work Harder

While the rewards may be individual, the steps of involvement tend to follow a common pattern. That is, one charitable act leads to another, and soon enough we want our contributions to count more, to be strategic. Once unleashed, however, the impulse to give has a way of running ahead of any plan. While that often signifies dedication and enthusiasm (definitely a good thing), it also typically leads to unproductive results or unintended consequences (not so hot).

In the past few years, for example, an organization launched by movie and TV actor Gary Sinise, star of hit show *CSI: NY*, has delivered more than $1 million in supplies to Iraqi schoolchildren—with more on the way. Yet this began, as so much philanthropy does, by mere chance.

A longtime supporter of American troops even before his best-known role as Lieutenant Dan, the Vietnam vet with a disability, in *Forrest Gump*, Sinise was on his second USO tour in Iraq in 2003. During an unscheduled visit to a school that American soldiers had helped rebuild, he recalls, "I saw the warm-hearted, healthy interactions among the Iraqi kids and teachers and the troops. I wanted to support that good feeling. I got the idea on the spot to send school supplies to the troops that had taken me to visit, so they could give them to the kids." In January 2004, he sent the first twenty-five boxes to the soldiers.

That was the germ of Operation Iraqi Children (OIC), which Sinise soon cofounded with Laura Hillenbrand, author of *Seabiscuit: An American Legend*. "I envisioned a much broader program that could ease the sting of what happens in war," he says. "I wanted an avenue to contribute." The partnership with Hillenbrand, too, was serendipity. A major on the ground in Iraq who had met Hillenbrand and Sinise individually suggested the two team up because of shared interests.

"Philanthropic plans start with visions, or goals—some very high level, sometimes almost breathless ('a better world'). But in a disciplined process, plans must drill down to specific tactics that can be implemented, tested, and monitored," explains Philip Cubeta, a financial services executive who writes a blog for donors, GiftHub.org. So it was with Sinise.

Shortly after the first school-supply shipment, and as publicity and donations rose, Sinise realized he needed help, not to mention a reliable distribution pipeline. That support materialized in the form of People to People International, a group led by Mary Eisenhower, whose grandfather, President Dwight D. Eisenhower, had founded the organization in 1956. And these days, OIC has mushroomed into a full-fledged charity. "We've had dozens and dozens of organizations in schools, businesses and individuals around the country participate in the programs," says

Sinise. "Since my initial contribution, we've also done collection programs at my kids' high school." To maintain goodwill, shipments from the Kansas City, Missouri, People to People warehouse are sent to American troops so that they can personally deliver the supplies, just as they did with Sinise's original shipment.

At last count, OIC had delivered nearly 1,300 boxes, including over 220,000 school-supply kits, more than half a million toys, thousands of pairs of shoes, thousands of backpacks, and more than fifty boxes of sports equipment.

Acting on impulse will work fine for a while, so long as you step back before the organization or your investment goes off the rails. Rather than feeling frustrated because your efforts end up foundering, JPMorgan Chase advisor Ringgold suggests that would-be givers take the time to establish benchmarks for success beforehand. Consider what will make you feel you've made that difference. Is it a certain amount of money raised for the organization you believe in? Is it building awareness in the community or in the media? Is it a small step on the road to discovering a

Eight Strategies to Begin Giving

As you get started, keep these strategies in mind. They were developed by Martha Taylor, who, along with Sondra Shaw-Hardy, founded the Women's Philanthropy Institute at the Center on Philanthropy at Indiana University.

1. **Start philanthropy as early in life as possible.** Even if you can't give as much as you'd like, your gifts will add up and begin to form your legacy.

2. **Find your passion and focus your gifts rather than scattering them.** Think about two or three areas of interest or causes you want to support, and make this your philanthropic mission. Not only will your gifts have more impact, but your giving will be more fulfilling.

3. **Work for parity in giving in your household.** You and your partner or other family members should have equal say about which causes your contributions support and how much to give.

4. **If you can, give out of your assets, which will contribute over time, rather than impulsively writing a check now and again.** Think of your philanthropy as you would a child, your investment in the future of our world.

5. **Consider the strength of numbers.** Organize with others to provide a pooled gift that can make a larger-scale project possible.

6. **Leverage your giving.** Increase your impact by challenging others to support the causes you hold dear.

7. **Teach the art of philanthropy to the next generation.** Instill in your children and the young people you associate with the values you treasure and your commitment to supporting them.

8. **Have fun with your philanthropy.** Celebrate your birthday with a philanthropic gift that you might not have thought possible. Surprise your friends by giving in their names—or to a nonprofit of their choice.

cure, which means you've engaged the interest of a research institution? Set a benchmark you can accomplish.

From Charity to Philanthropy, Making a Plan

People who are considering ongoing contributions often find it helpful to draft a giving plan, perhaps in consultation with a financial advisor or a philanthropy consultant, who can help them identify where to invest resources, evaluate priorities, and sort through financial options (see Chapter 8 for more on working with advisors). Eventually, you might make a long-term commitment to establishing a legacy, an estate plan, or some other vehicle that engages the next generation (see Chapter 10). "Ultimately," says Ringgold, "donors realize that figuring out how to make their efforts count leads to a continuous learning curve, as well as ongoing personal rewards."

Ann Lurie has traveled just that path, which had some rough twists and turns. In 2007, Lurie pledged a staggering $108 million to charity, both privately and through her Chicago-based Ann and Robert H. Lurie Foundation, which earned her the number-fifteen ranking on the *Chronicle of Philanthropy*'s annual list of the fifty most generous Americans (her third time making the list). "Long before I had a checkbook for what's described as 'transformational philanthropy,' I learned at a young age that being helpful in some way to someone who needs help can produce a lot of personal gratification," she says. "My mother said I should do a good deed daily, and she gave me some examples. So I started doing that at a fairly young age. It was the high point of my day."

In the mid-eighties, Lurie, a registered nurse, and her husband, Robert, partner and one-time college roommate of real estate investment baron Sam Zell, began thinking about philanthropy in a structured way. After setting up the foundation, they came up with a list of general areas to support. Then, in 1988, Robert contracted colon cancer. He died two years later. "We were partners," says Lurie. "After we heard the diagnosis, I went home and had a total bawl-out. It's been many years and it's still painful." With six children— "my youngest was five"—Lurie determined to carry on.

Over the years, she has expanded the list she and her husband began. "Primarily, I've chosen causes that stir me in some way and that also make me think my contributions can make a difference. It's not always the case that they can." Today, Lurie focuses on two areas. Last year, she committed $100 million to build a children's hospital in Chicago. She also does extensive work in Africa. Not only has she founded Aid Village Clinics, which provides health care to 90,000 people in southeast Kenya, but she has also built schools in Ethiopia and sponsored twenty-five Masai youngsters through high school and college. "I like to stay around and watch the evolution of the changes I've been able to make," she says.

IT STARTS WITH KIDS

"My mother said I should do a good deed daily, and she gave me some examples. So I started doing that at a fairly young age. It was the high point of my day."
—ANN LURIE, CHICAGO PHILANTHROPIST

Her children go their own way. None

of the six, now grown, work with her, but each has established his or her own foundation. "I don't think kids should have to carry on the parents' philanthropy," she says. "They should be able to do what's interesting to them individually."

Through it all, Lurie's childhood habit has remained. "I walk a lot," she says. "I often see people wringing their hands over a map on Michigan Avenue. So I walk up to them, say I live here and ask if I can help. You get so much gratification from pointing people in the right direction—just like righting things on a bigger scale."

A Giving Plan Built on Career Skills

There are countless others who make the kind of commitment Lurie has, yet with a fraction of her resources. Oseola McCarty may have been unusual, but she is hardly alone.

Faith Ralston, for example, runs her own executive coaching consultancy in Minneapolis. Seeing a need in the market—and presumably in the culture as well—she developed a leadership-training program for women that she calls Play to Your Strengths. Ralston teaches the program's precepts at local business colleges and coaches clients one-on-one.

Some years ago, while meeting with a networking group of five other professional women, the executive coach stumbled on a technique that seemed to unleash energy and women's inner voices. Basically, the group called out possible career paths, on-the-job options, or potential goals and asked each woman to speak to those. "Our eyes lit up whenever something was important to us," says Ralston. "Getting the group members to talk that way, off the cuff and spontaneously, is a way to trick the brain."

She began leading free workshops for various women's groups, encouraging participants to form their own small "Circles" in order to further their goals. In 2003, with a few partners, Ralston then launched the nonprofit Awesome Women, which offers workshop dinners (with a modest per-person fee to cover food and the venue) that help women "speak up and move toward what they want in life, home or work." The event also provides a network for creating additional Awesome Women Circles that will maintain the support. "Saying it out loud and hearing what you said back from other people reinforces the belief that you can actually do it," says Ralston. Awesome Women has been operating on only $10,000 a year, though Ralston is looking for funding to enlarge the operation to more communities.

David Richard Gives Away Wheelchairs—and Mobilizes Thousands

In the end, philanthropists are not defined by the size of their gifts but by the reach of their spirit and strategy. David Richard, founder of the grassroots Wheels for Humanity (WFH), certainly understands that.

Headquartered in a 10,800-square-foot warehouse in North Hollywood, Wheels for Humanity refurbishes used wheelchairs to ship overseas to people who can't afford one. Volunteers do most of the work. "I'm good at getting wheelchairs to people, but I never learned to ask for money," says Richard.

Begun in Richard's garage in 1996, WFH grew out of efforts by his brother Mark. On a visit to Guatemala in the mid-eighties, Mark Richard saw a woman with a disability by the side of the road who got around by dragging herself along by her elbows. Then thirty-one, the woman had been paralyzed by polio at age seven. Mark returned weeks later with used wheelchairs for the woman and eighteen other people with disabilities.

Inspired, David Richard, then a sales manager for a golf-supply company, began collecting and repairing wheelchairs. He took 160 refurbished chairs to Guatemala late in 1995. The next year, Richard incorporated WFH as a 501(c)(3) charity, and he's been at it, full-time, ever since, accepting only a small salary.

In the United States, new wheelchairs start at $300 or so, and thousands are discarded each year. Worldwide, an estimated 120 million people with disabilities need mobile chairs, but the average household income in developing countries is less than $1,000 a year. So millions of people with disabilities must spend their lives lying down, unable to move around. WFH says it can fit and deliver a chair for only $120.

To date, WFH has fitted more than 42,000 chairs for kids

and adults with disabilities in sixty-six countries. As the organization continues to grow, its Los Angeles location is handy. Over the years, Tim Allen and Ali MacGraw have joined WFH's advisory council, and David Hasselhoff, Goldie Hawn, and Robin Williams have been donors. Rocker Rod Stewart is a longtime volunteer. Yet WFH operates largely on a shoestring. Even after joining LA's family of United Cerebral Palsy organizations in January 2007 to ramp up its reach and impact, WFH remains a tightly run, predominantly volunteer organization, with a scant annual budget of less than $2 million.

But for Richard, finding chairs and shipping them to remote Mongolia or Zimbabwe isn't the tough part. There are lots of dusty chairs around, and carriers and airlines usually donate their services. The heart-wrenching part is ensuring that every chair fits the needs of its new owner. "Few agencies specialize in seating and custom-fitting," he says. "There are all these services and groups that send chairs overseas thinking one size fits all. But you can't just buy a chair for $50 and drop it off for someone who's never been measured. It's complicated to tailor a pediatric chair for a four-year-old with cerebral palsy."

A WFH team—typically Richard and volunteer physical therapists, doctors, and chair mechanics, plus a board member or two, maybe, or a Paralympic athlete—travels wherever a container of chairs is shipped. The team runs an on-site rehabilitation clinic, providing physical therapy and custom fitting for users.

"But just fitting the chair is really a Band-Aid," says

Richard. "I want to have enough funding to build physical therapy facilities with the latest technology, trained staff and handbooks translated into the language of every country—Ukrainian, Spanish, Vietnamese. In the meantime, we're doing good work without a lot of money."

Chapter 3

WHAT DO YOU CARE ABOUT?

IDENTIFYING YOUR CAUSE

The world and its communities are overflowing with need. One look around reveals no dearth of deserving causes. At last count, the IRS listed nearly 1.7 million charities with legally established nonprofit status in the United States. That's double the number of twenty-five years ago, representing a growth rate twice that of the business sector.

In addition, up until 2007, thousands of worthy not-for-profits weren't even required to register with the IRS. Small organizations with less than $5,000 in gross annual receipts, such as neighborhood associations, PTAs, or community theater companies, didn't need to file any paperwork to gain tax-exempt status, although some did. The roughly 300,000 religious congregations in the country still don't need to register, although about half do so voluntarily.

As of the 2007 tax year (2008 filing), however, the IRS is requiring small charities with revenues of $25,000 or less to file a new short form so that the government can better track nonprofits. Even so, this new form, the 990-N or e-Postcard, covers little more than the charity's address, revenue, and top staff. Plus, organizations are permitted to skip filing in the first few years without penalty, presumably until everyone gets adjusted.

All in all, there are millions of nonprofits out there that are actively seeking your dollars and support, with no centralized way for potential donors to unearth what groups address which issues or causes.

If You Had $1 Million to Give Away, Where Should It Go?

As a result, trying to choose your cause is not particularly well served by hunting for that supremely special, really deserving organization. In truth, there are thousands of them. Or, put the other way around, no totally perfect group exists. The most honorable, effective, dedicated, and ethical organizations also make some mistakes and suffer glitches. How could they not? Like every human endeavor, nonprofits are prone to the exigencies of time and circumstance—and, no doubt, also to some incompetence and bad actors. In addition, charities take on the world's toughest, longest-running problems and, as you well know, such challenges throw up stubborn obstacles that will not be cleared either this year or the next. Solving social ills, supporting a talented arts group, or sponsoring a promising student takes work and commitment. To further complicate matters, nonprofits are proliferating so fast that many groups now have overlapping missions and focus on similar issues. For example, consider the universe of funding directed at finding a cure for breast cancer or AIDS. An online search for "AIDS charities" turns up some 36,000 results. It's hard to know where to begin.

For the majority of would-be donors, then, figuring out where to engage and whether they can or will have an impact is, at best, confusing and, at worst, downright discouraging.

Katherina Rosqueta refers to this predicament as "the million-dollar question." In other words, if you had $1 million to give away and wanted to make the biggest possible difference, where should you put it?

As executive director of the Center for High Impact Philanthropy at the University of Pennsylvania, a research group founded in 2006 by a few alumni of the university's Wharton School, Rosqueta and a staff of six are looking into "smarter philanthropy." That is, the practices and methods of philanthropy that will work best. The center has targeted urban education in the United States as its debut arena to study, because Rosqueta and many advisors believe that's where strategic philanthropy can do the most long-term good. Inarguably, investing in education has proved to yield enduring dividends for individuals, communities, future generations, and society at large. So since launch, the center's staff and associates have been surveying schools, programs, and charities around the country to come up with objective measures and facts about what effectively improves outcomes for disadvantaged kids—what truly creates positive results?

On the face of it, then, the center's innovative work would seem a keen resource to tap when kicking off the quest for that million-dollar donation. With its rigorous, well-funded, well-focused mission, you'd think its executive director would be eager to tell us exactly where to make our contribution to education in order to get the most bang for our buck. But she isn't.

Sure, says Rosqueta, once the center's field research is sorted out and weighed over the next few years, she'll be able to point to some high-level things that work and some other things that don't. She'll be able to offer advice about addressing education's deep challenges, including the role of competition, the need for better teachers, the pros and cons of school vouchers, and so on. But in the end, says Rosqueta, categorically, "There is no silver bullet. The one place to spend a million dollars doesn't exist. These are difficult problems and if you really want to have an impact you have to learn and keep learning relentlessly." In lesser ways, the dilemma holds with $1,000 or $100, too.

As a coda to our giving parable, Rosqueta invokes one of the most admired stars in the philanthropy firmament: "I was in the room when Warren Buffett gave his money to Bill Gates," she says. "He said he was giving it to the Gates Foundation because giving away money is so much harder than making money"—and Buffett believes the Gateses will make the smartest, best use of his extraordinary gift.

You hear a similar theme expressed by experienced phi-

Why the Wealthy Give to Charity

In an annual national survey of wealthy Americans:

♦ nearly 90 percent said the primary reason they give to charity is that they believe in specific causes and have a desire to "give back" to society

♦ 80 percent said they hoped to teach their children that wealth brings "social responsibilities"

♦ those with philanthropic intentions said they were most likely to contribute to

68 percent, academic institutions and 66 percent, health-related groups

43 percent, religious groups

39 percent, libraries or museums

36 percent, environmental or public-policy groups

2007 U.S. Trust Survey of Affluent Americans

lanthropists, fund-raising consultants and, indeed, by the Gates Foundation itself. Patty Stonesifer, who stepped down in September 2008 as chief executive of the Bill & Melinda Gates Foundation to become chair of the Smithsonian Institution, was well known for managing expectations for the Gateses' philanthropic largesse. One of the biggest charitable foundations in the world, the Bill & Melinda Gates Foundation had assets worth nearly $39 billion in 2007, and, with Buffett's infusion, assets are estimated to eventually reach a staggering $60 billion or so. Yet Stonesifer routinely put that in perspective. "The Gates Foundation spends $400 million a year to try to get kids ready for college in the U.S.," she has said. "The state of California spends $40 billion. So our money is just a drop in the bucket."

Bottom Line from Banker Carla Harris: "It's a Joy"

"I'm always asked how I do so much, but nobody ever asks why," says Carla Ann Harris. "It's because of how much I enjoy it. I have a passion for helping other people. It's a joy."

Managing directors at prominent banking firms like Morgan Stanley don't often look like Carla Harris. In her mid-forties, Harris is invariably the only black woman in the room when the firm's biggest deals get done. In 1999, she steered the bonanza $5.5 billion public offering for UPS, which at the time was the largest in U.S. history. Among dozens of accolades, she has been named by *Fortune* magazine as one of the fifty most powerful black executives in America. "My family had a drive for education," says Harris, who grew up an only child in Jacksonville, Florida. Her mother was an assistant dean at a middle school, while her father captained a commercial fishing boat. "They stressed that you should achieve the highest goals you could. And then go above and beyond"—which is just what Harris has done.

With a partial scholarship, she mostly worked her way through Harvard, graduating magna cum laude in economics. A Wall Street summer internship, arranged by Sponsors for Educational Opportunity (SEO), a nonprofit that mentors students of color, put her on the financial services track. She went on to earn an MBA at Harvard Business School, with distinguished second-years honors, and has been setting records at Morgan Stanley ever since. Asked if all these hard-charging accomplishments are just a wee bit wearying, Harris only laughs: "It's not at all stressful. I have the brains and energy to do well. I feel like I'm doing what I was supposed to do."

Harris still finds time to speak to students around the country, instilling ambition and hope. "There aren't a lot of women or folks of color doing what I do, so it's important to show young people an example ahead of them." She also mentors young people and uses her expertise to build nonprofits.

After thirteen-hour days on Wall Street, she frequently heads up to Harlem to pursue her second passion: gospel singing. Evenings and weekends, Harris sings with the choir at St. Charles Borromeo Catholic Church. This is hardly a banker's holiday. She's been billed at the Apollo Theater and Lincoln Center. She has funded and coproduced two CDs of her performances, *Carla's First Christmas* and *Joy Is Waiting*.

Like any astute investment banker, Harris has a plan. She established a small scholarship fund in 1990 at her alma mater, Bishop Kenny High School, in Jacksonville. "Many African American parents who send their kids to private Catholic elementary schools can't afford high school, because the tuition goes up four or five times. That's not true in New York, but it's true in Jacksonville and elsewhere." So as her singing career gains traction, Harris is upping the ante on her giving. "I really turbocharged the fund in 2000 when I released my first album," she says. "If you can directly impact someone's life by enabling access to education, it has a multiplier effect. If you do well in society, you do well for others."

Through her singing, Harris has pledged to raise $500,000 for two schools that mean a lot to her. At last count, she was close to her goal. Half will go to Bishop Kenny and half to the school run by St. Charles Borromeo. "Hopefully, I motivate the people I'm helping," she says. "This is what you must do. It's the rent you pay for being here. It's as necessary as breathing."

How to Tell You've Found What You're Looking For

Join a mission that directly and deeply engages you, whether that's working in the arts, advocating for single moms, raising the bar on education, legislating for consensus to ease global warming, helping to eradicate malaria in Kenya, delivering clean water in the favelas of Rio de Janeiro, building homes for Americans who can't afford one, volunteering as a hospice worker, nurturing abandoned children, or anything else. The list is as long as you choose to make it. The stories of need are as heartrending and critical today as they will be tomorrow. One more time: just jump in.

"My philosophy about philanthropy is that it's not just dollars, but it's about having a passion about giving something back, about doing something that helps society," says Sandy Weill, who has been credited as the architect and guiding force in building Citigroup. Weill has given away more than a staggering $500 million of his own money since the 1970s and, after officially retiring from Citigroup in 2006, now is a full-time philanthropist—"the third act," as he puts it.

Among a bevy of high-impact efforts, Weill is perhaps best known for his fund-raising and board work in rescuing New York's legendary Carnegie Hall and for establishing the Joan and Sanford I. Weill Medical College at Cornell University. He's also been instrumental in launching a branch of Cornell's medical school in Qatar, the first overseas school to confer an American medical degree. Largely because of Sandy's wife, Joan, and her commitment to modern dance, the Weills are also the primary funders of the Joan Weill Center for Dance, a gleaming eight-story building on the west side of Manhattan, home to the Alvin Ailey Dance Company.

Like the Weills do, it's worthwhile to keep your emotions front and center when selecting your cause. Don't discount your depth of feeling or your instincts about a cause or an organization. Many nonprofits and charities try to prove their case to potential donors with a barrage of rational metrics and impersonal analysis. If you give only because you succumb to the latest request you receive or because a friend is persistent, it's odds-on your interest will fade. While results should and can be measured, and successful outcomes are critical, remember, it's passion that will fuel your philanthropic journey.

The Cause that Found
Astrid Heger

For many people, the intensity of need or the pain of injustice means that the cause chooses you, rather than the other way around. That's how it was for Dr. Astrid Heger.

It may seem unthinkable today, but in 1983, when Heger, a pediatrician, volunteered to work at Los Angeles County Hospital + USC Medical Center, she learned that children who had been sexually abused were physically examined not once but over and over again so that experts could testify about the injuries at multiple court hearings. Heger was outraged by the unnecessary and added trauma. She was incensed by how often such cases were lost anyway because the "evidence" was so subjective. "At the time, people didn't want to believe sexual abuse was happening, and many cases weren't prosecuted," says Heger, whose cool blond looks belie her fiery determination. "There was no science or documentation. Anybody could say anything." In reaction, Heger pioneered the use of photographic documentation and rigorous methods of evaluation so that kids would be physically examined only once.

In 1984, her efforts paid off, setting a legal precedent in California and, over time, creating new standards in state after state, across the country. "Scientific documentation brought authenticity to the investigation and allowed cases to go forward," she says. From there, with only a trickle of funding and no salary or staff, Heger began treating vulnerable children in a temporary clinic, an abandoned trailer located on the medical center's parking lot. Authorities kept warning her off. "One administrator told me to cease and desist because building programs to deliver services for women and children was not a priority." Heger's soft voice gets even quieter. "It amused me to drive my truck around that guy," she says triumphantly.

Over the years, social workers, counselors, and police officers kept bringing her more and more victims of family violence. There was nowhere else to go. "Against all odds," says Heger, "I decided to methodically build a system that would deliver quality care, and demonstrate to bureaucrats that keeping families together instead of in jails could create an economic model that would save money for the system."

In 2001, Heger's programs officially became the LAC + USC Medical Center's Violence Intervention Program (VIP), which then went on to raise $2 million and move into a renovated facility in 2003. Nowadays, with an operating budget of upward of $11 million, mostly from Los Angeles

FINDING PURPOSE

"We see big trends occurring in the world of philanthropy and it's having a big impact. Most of all the new earned money is part of this trend. People are including philanthropy in their life plans. They're saying, 'I've accomplished a lot and what I want to do in the time remaining is make a difference. I really want to do something to make this a better world with the time and resources I've got.'"
—Robert Ottenhof, CEO, GuideStar

County government contracts, VIP is a one-stop care center that annually evaluates more than 20,000 victims of family violence, sexual assault, and elder abuse.

In her mid-sixties, divorced, and mother to three grown sons, Heger runs VIP, teaches, writes books, and has been showered with awards. She often testifies as an expert witness in high-impact court cases and is regularly sought out by the media because of her expertise on matters of rape and other violent crimes. She also serves as a consultant to the coroner on sexual assault and child death cases. But she's far from satisfied with her accomplishments.

"It absolutely infuriates me that the women and kids who are victims of assault or abuse are invisible and don't have a voice," says Heger. "My dad began as a child laborer in the steel mills in England and eventually became a college professor. He taught me to live your life to make a difference."

As America ages, Heger also sees another crisis looming. "We're seeing more and more elders abused," she says. "I've treated a ninety-year-old woman who had been tied to her chair for three days while caretakers ransacked her home looking for money. She was alert then, but now she's demented and alone. There's nothing in place to protect her." The California Department of Social Services estimates that about 40,000 reported cases of elder abuse occur in Los Angeles County each year. The total is estimated to be up to five times higher. "Most people don't want to look at this," says Heger. "They look down the road and think, 'That could be me.' They'd rather not think about it. But how do we protect our elderly and make them feel valuable?"

For Heger, success is measured only by how effectively VIP stops violence and helps victims. "You're not allowed to use Medicaid to pay for things victims need, like cosmetic surgery and orthodontia so kids can smile again after their faces have been beaten to a pulp for years. That money also can't be used for transportation to school or for taxi vouchers to get victims home or for a prom dress to make a girl feel successful." In response, VIP supporters have launched HEART (Helping Ease Abuse-Related Trauma), a volunteer group that privately raises about $100,000 a year for such family needs. "We're the only center that does that," says Heger, still tilting at the system. Her dad would be proud.

"There's no question that I work in a very dark place. But there are people who get it and make it possible to grow new programs and build new things. I hear about acts of horrible meanness and violation and abuse every day. But it's the acts of kindness that really make me weep."

Audition Organizations and Ask Questions

To make your efforts count, take stock of what you care about most. Take some time to research the area you're interested in giving to—say, six months or so. Explore a few organizations before committing dollars or serious energy.

Invariably, when choosing a cause, people build on personal experiences, and as we well know, biographies vary. For example, billionaire David Koch, executive vice president of the privately owned Koch Industries, which reels in $98 billion in yearly revenue, is known as the second wealthiest resident of New York City. He and his three brothers are all survivors of prostate cancer. As a result, Koch not only funds research for its cure but also stays close to work in the field. "I identify where outstanding cancer research is taking place, where the leading researchers and programs are, and that's where I give money," he says, listing New York's Memorial Sloan-Kettering Cancer Center, Houston's M. D. Anderson Cancer Center, and Baltimore's Johns Hopkins as a few of his grantees. In 2007, in one of the largest-ever contributions for prostate cancer research, Koch donated $5 million to the Prostate Cancer Foundation to create a cross-discipline team to search for a cure.

A chemical engineer with two degrees from Massachusetts Institute of Technology, Koch also focuses on science, sitting on the boards of the Smithsonian National Museum of Natural History in Washington, D.C., and the American Museum of Natural History in New York. In 2006, his $20 million gift helped refurbish the latter's famous dinosaur displays—now housed in the David H. Koch Dinosaur Wing—which he had first visited as a child with his father in the 1950s. And in 2008, Koch pledged a staggering $100 million gift to renovate the New York State Theater at Lincoln Center—the largest private capital donation in the center's history.

With such enormous resources to offer, Koch gets a slew of requests. But he's learned to focus on the causes most meaningful to him and, more important, he makes sure his contributions have the impact he intends. Too often, non-profits large and small do a poor job of communicating their vision and plans and of inviting volunteers and donors to participate in decision making. "There are so many worthy organizations out there doing good things," says Koch, explaining how he makes his choices. "I focus on the ones that are well managed and really talented." For instance, when the Lincoln Center gift was announced in July 2008, Koch mentioned in a press interview that he'd been attending the New York State Theater for forty years and would not have made a contribution of that magnitude unless he were convinced that "the quality of the work was world-class."

You need to audition organizations as much as you do the mission.

Remember, too, that identifying philanthropic goals is inextricably tied to assessing results. In choosing the cause that speaks to you, look at both sides of the equation: how much it needs your help, and what you and the group can actually get done.

"Anyone can make difference," says Kathy LeMay, founder of Raising Change, a Northampton, Massachusetts-based fund-raising consultancy. "If you don't have money, you shouldn't think you can't make a difference." Having grown up poor with a single mom, LeMay understands this very well. She began her career in philanthropy by working with women survivors of the siege and rape-genocide camps in war-torn Yugoslavia.

Today, LeMay is a consultant who works with wealthy

individuals to help them find their philanthropic mission, and with nonprofits to raise capital—"I don't call it philanthropy consulting; I call it social action planning." She is adamant about the need for open communication among donors and organizations: "If the nonprofit staff keeps saying how great things are and just paints a pretty picture,

Q&A: Discover Your "Spiritual Money"

A legacy planner, Barbara Culver runs a financial advisory firm called Resonate, Inc., based in Cincinnati. Years ago, she began providing what she calls values-based financial planning, because she felt that the conventional approaches of money managers do not uncover what people really want or need. Here, Culver explains the goals and process of her version of financial planning.

Q: *In your experience, what's missing from the traditional approach?*
Culver: I was trained as a financial advisor. That means you talk about financial needs based on the premise that you don't want to run out of money before you run out of breath. So I was trained to focus only on tax-efficient methods of wealth transfer. But life is about more than that.

Q: *What is "values-based planning?"*
Culver: The first thing I do for values-based planning is talk about the five dimensions of money—its financial, emotional, spiritual, psychological and physical possibilities. Then I talk about how, as human beings, we're all way more alike than we are different, no matter our age, lifestyles or gender. Each life is built on those same

five components—financial, emotional, spiritual, psychological and physical. People get that. Money reflects the same five dimensions that we have in our day-to-day lives.

Q: *How does this approach change the conversation?*

Culver: The key difference is intention. Depending on our behavior, money can connect or disconnect us. When I describe the different dimensions of money, people begin to talk about what's of value to them and the kind of questions that keep them up at night rather than what the advisor considers important. You find out what people want you to address and there's a cumulative effect. They begin to think about money and wealth with a broader perspective, to understand how it can advance their purpose in life, the lessons they've learned. Almost invariably, they begin to see that the highest and best use of money is spiritual, or giving.

Q: *How do you uncover these emotional and psychological dimensions?*

Culver: Besides a lot of listening, we've developed tools and questionnaires that lead people to get clear. I always say that if they prefer a more traditional approach, they probably should work with another advisor.

Q: *What's the ultimate goal?*

Culver: My job is to help clients get clear about their emotional and psychological attitudes to money when they plug in the financial decisions. I want people to feel comfortable around the whole subject of money, so they can be confident about how much will be enough for the family. Then they can align their money with their values. That gets to the next phase—philanthropic giving and the impact you can make with a particular organization.

there's no chance for a good partnership." Such rosy predictions benefit no one. Instead, she says, you need the organization to provide specific and sincere details. "Say to them, 'Walk me through it. Show me the impact. Educate me on what you know so I get it.' Then, later, when it looks like we're not solving the problem fast enough, there won't be disappointment."

Donor education takes time and honesty, says LeMay, underscoring that this is difficult for nonprofits, because they're used to trying to please donors and keep contributions in the pipeline. "But nonprofits need to take the time to teach donors what we know," she says. If an organization can't or won't educate you or demonstrate impact, then, says LeMay, "you may care about the cause, but you ought to find a different organization."

Diana Barrett Learned from a Beginner's Mistakes

Finding philanthropic focus takes time and practice. People who have been through the process say it's about trial and error. It's also not uncommon for new volunteers or donors to discover that a cause or an organization turns out to be the wrong match, and they need to move on. Despite having more resources than most and a meticulous plan, that's what happened to Diana Barrett.

Brainy and accomplished, Barrett has had a career in public health policy, teaching at both the Harvard Business

School and its School of Public Health. She focused on business leadership in the social sector and how public-private partnerships can reduce poverty and disease, particularly HIV/AIDS. "I felt seriously that you're only on earth for a limited time and this is not a dress rehearsal," she says. "You need to work to change the world while you're in it."

Her mother was wealthy, and that made life in Boston with three kids and her husband, Bob Vila, the home-improvement TV star, more comfortable. Yet Barrett made serious efforts to hide her money, down to being self-conscious about the car she drove. "I had to be careful how I positioned myself, as an academic," she says. "Women had a hard enough time. A wealthy woman would have been dismissed as a dilettante." A few times a year, Barrett would write charitable checks, often to Paul Farmer's well-known organization Partners in Health, which provides medical care in developing areas. "But I was essentially just giving away money," she says. "I wasn't putting it to work."

Years before, on the advice of a lawyer, she and her mother had set up a small private foundation that was administered by a larger community foundation. Like so many of the family foundations established in that generation, its sole purpose was tax savings. No one in the family was interested in learning about giving. No one had ever assessed the money's potential.

Then, in 2004, Barrett's mother died, and the foundation's assets jumped from a few million dollars to $28 million. "That made it a serious proposition," says Barrett. Around the same time, she and Vila, whose kids were grown, decided to move to New York. She turned to philanthropy full-time, helped by a colleague she hired. Unsurprisingly, given her background, Barrett began looking at "pockets of poverty in New York's five boroughs," with the idea of providing social services and health care. "My mother was Hispanic, and my husband is Cuban. We have an adopted Colombian daughter. I wanted to be relevant for the huge Hispanic community here."

For more than a year, Barrett and her associate researched, made field visits, and ran neighborhood ZIP code screens, looking for incidences of asthma, nutritional deficiencies, and other indicators of where their efforts would most count. Ultimately, she says, "we decided that funding organizations that combat such problems wasn't worth it." Why? "Nonprofits fight for every dollar and they're highly autonomous. They don't want to share plans or play in the same sandbox with other organizations. There's an inbred fear and dislike of collaborating. We thought we'd be wasting our time and money."

Nobody said philanthropy was perfect.

Soon after, "out of the blue," a friend asked Barrett to look at an assembly cut, or early version, of a documentary called *Born Into Brothels*, with an eye to offering funding. "It was a sea change, a paradigm shift," she says. "I realized that telling a great story was a better way to raise awareness and address an issue, especially if it was in a movie that people want to sit through." The film went on to win an Oscar for best documentary in 2005.

Barrett shifted gears. Today her foundation, Fledgling

Fund, supports media projects "that target entrenched social problems." Recent grantees include filmmakers who produced an Emmy-award-winning documentary about Abu Ghraib, the prison near Baghdad where American soldiers abused Iraqi prisoners. Another film, about ethnic rape in the Congo, won an award at the Sundance Film Festival.

A recent Barrett project, *Very Young Girls*, follows a number of young women who became prostitutes in New York City. One fourteen-year-old is lured from her home, beaten, raped, held captive, and sold for sex. When found by the police, the teen—not the male customer—is arrested. Men who have sex with underage girls are supposed to be criminally prosecuted, but the law has a loophole: if the child accepts money for sex, the man becomes a john and, as such, is usually simply fined. Legally, the child becomes the criminal. "Today, the average age of entry into prostitution in the U.S. is thirteen," says Barrett. "The law is insane, and I hope to change it." The film was an official selection at the 2007 Toronto International Film Festival.

To leverage the influence of such films, Barrett has developed her own model. She chooses an issue she thinks important and provides "finishing funds," or the last bridge needed to complete a project. "First funds are too risky," she says. Grantee filmmakers are required to write a statement about what kind of impact their film can make. They must also produce a trailer so that the film can be advertised and marketed. Barrett then mounts an outreach effort, offering, for example, free screenings to nonprofits and advocacy groups, which function as fund-raisers and build awareness.

These days, with ZIP code scans well behind her, her foundation assets valued at $25 million or so, and a few additional staff members, Barrett says, "I believe an emotional driver is important to create change. But you need more than charisma or passion. You need to find the real experts and leaders in the field and be strategic." She adds, "I'm always annoyed by the phrase 'giving away money,' because you don't make a difference with money alone. You need to invest in a community and get to know it. You've got to put in time in the trenches and go to board meetings and understand the organization you're funding."

Chapter 4

HOW MUCH SHOULD YOU GIVE?

BALANCING YOUR INTEREST AND GIFTS

Deciding how much to give, perhaps the most delicate issue in the philanthropic pantheon, is of course a most personal choice. But there are some hard-and-fast rules: Never feel pushed into giving more than you intend. Never be influenced by guilt. Never make a decision based on someone else's gift.

On average, Americans give 2 to 4 percent of their income to charity, although many people, not only the rich, give a whole lot more. Unsurprisingly, high–net worth households have the greatest impact. They are responsible for two-thirds of all household charity in the country, according to a recent survey of more than 30,000 house-holds in high–net worth neighborhoods across the country conducted for Bank of America by the Center on Philanthropy at Indiana University. The survey defined

"By age 35, I had given away 100 percent of my $1 million inheritance and [I] have now given away $1 million more simply by earning $100,000 or more each year and giving away 40 percent to 50 percent per year over twenty years. It adds up to wonderful relationships and change making."
—Tracy Gary, founder, Inspired Legacies

high–net worth households as those with annual incomes of at least $200,000 or assets of at least $1 million.

Still, there appears to be a lot of untapped potential. While average total giving for the study's high–net worth respondents came to nearly an impressive $121,000 annually, the median annual total was just over $16,000. In other words, a few big-ticket donors pulled up the average. More tellingly, that $121,000 sum drops to about $83,000 when you factor out the money that went into tax-saving vehicles like foundations and donor-advised funds (see Chapter 6). Therefore, most of the money won't be given away for years. Some critics refer to this money as being "parked" for tax and estate-planning purposes.

More Generosity Now Means Greater Impact Later

People with even more money seem to give proportionately less, according to another recent study, by an unusual organization called the New Tithing Group.

Claude Rosenberg, who died in 2008 at age eighty, launched this San Francisco–based private foundation in the late 1990s. He had earned a fortune as a fund manager and spent the last decades of his life trying to persuade wealthy people to increase their charitable giving and thus whittle their tax bill. Rosenberg argued that charitable giving is limited because most Americans—and, pointedly, the wealthiest ones—make donations based on a percentage of income. Instead, all of us, or so he thought, could easily afford to give more if we paid closer attention to personal financial and tax planning, thereby reckoning our giving capacity based on net worth rather than yearly income. If net worth were the yardstick, claimed Rosenberg, a lot of the money that ends up going to pay estate and other taxes could be fueling nonprofit causes.

To make this case, he published a book in 1994 called *Wealthy and Wise: How You and America Can Get the Most Out of Your Giving*, and established the New Tithing Group, with a Web site that let visitors run computerized calculations to see what portion of their assets they could afford to donate and the resulting reduction in their taxes. (Since Rosenberg's death, the foundation and site have been dismantled.) Rosenberg also funded extensive research into public IRS data to unearth how much rich people actually donate. That's how he found that most charitable contributions conform to a percentage of income—which is what tax accountants and other financial advisors typically recommend. The research revealed that, relative to what they can afford, poor and middle-class people give more than the wealthy do.

In 2005, for example, New Tithing analysis found that taxpayers with incomes of $10 million or more and average assets of $125 million allocated only about 1.4 percent of their investable assets to charity. Rosenberg also uncovered what he called the "eyeballing-lowballing syndrome." That is, people of means frequently "eyeball" their incomes to decide how much to donate to charity. Since they make very rough guesses about what they can actually afford, they usually "lowball" their gifts.

But according to Rosenberg—and the sector advisors who've since adopted his arguments—giving more now likely yields significantly greater rewards for your chosen cause than waiting until you're older and perhaps richer, or until your estate makes a bequest in your will. That's because unaddressed social ills, as we all intuitively know, tend to worsen over time. Whatever problem you're trying to resolve is bound to turn more severe as time passes. Plus, the inevitable march of inflation means that today's dollar buys more value than tomorrow's dollar can. Even so, the majority of donors earmark the same amount for

How Much Do Americans Give at Any One Time?

♦ The average gift size is $172, about 8 percent of the estimated average total household contribution of $2,065 for a year.

♦ The median gift amount is $50.

♦ Two-thirds (66 percent) of gift amounts were below $100, and 45 percent were below $50.

November 2007, American Express Charitable Gift Survey, conducted by the Center on Philanthropy at Indiana University charity every year, without adjusting for the effects of inflation.

All in all, says the Rosenberg Rule, as some have dubbed it, the smart move is to give today rather than tomorrow.

Figuring Out How You Feel About Money

Despite that reasonable, common-sense approach, the reality of contributing money to charity can be complicated. We all bring individual agendas, histories, fantasies, expectations, and anxieties to our financial transactions—to spending and saving as much as to giving.

Money isn't merely the paper stuff we use to buy and sell things. It also represents emotions and values that we learn from our families and our circumstances and that we internalize as children. "We can't handle money responsibly until we understand what money means psychologically," says Annette Lieberman, a New York psychologist who specializes in conflicts about personal finances. "A good exercise," she says, "is to think about your earliest memory of money. It will tell you a lot about what you first learned about money growing up in your family and it will indicate how what you learned influences you today."

For example, sudden wealth is often not the all-purpose enabler that many people imagine it to be. Money can also immobilize its recipient. We've all heard sad tales about the people who win millions in a lottery and end up being destroyed because the money overwhelms their lives. Until such instant millionaires feel in control of their newfound wealth and, in many cases, discover the rewards of philanthropy, they frequently feel as if they don't deserve their good fortune. Here's a case in point.

Painful Lessons of Inheriting a Fortune as a Teenager

When Marian Moore was eighteen, her mother died, and the young woman suddenly came into a sizable family inheritance. Now in her mid-fifties with three grown kids and living in Minneapolis as a music producer and the founding president of a philanthropy consultancy, Moore speaks even today with palpable emotion about how the windfall paralyzed her. "It came before I was developed and it represented many generations of wealth."

Her great-grandfather was a pioneering corporate tycoon, while her parents were social activists. Her father, an Episcopal bishop, officiated at the well-known Cathedral Church of St. John the Divine in Upper Manhattan. "I understood privilege, but I didn't understand the depth of what that meant. When money comes from left field and it's an accident of birth, it takes time to accept it," says Moore. "My financial situation was based on a system where money divides people. I felt that emotionally."

Moore's wealth set her apart from friends and from potential boyfriends. "When the woman is the one with money, it's hard to process the experience. You have to figure out how to be with a man who has less money than you do."

It also kept her isolated from the group of New York artists she hung out with during her twenties. She would never, for instance, invite anyone to her home. That's because she lived in a comfortable apartment on New York's Upper East Side, while everyone she knew was scrambling just to pay the rent. She didn't want to be rejected by people she called friends.

The money weighed Moore down and made her feel guilty. She kept it a secret from everyone she knew. She remained, as she puts it, "in the closet" until age thirty-two, when she connected with the Tides Foundation in San Francisco, a group that helps the wealthy get comfortable with money and put their philanthropic instincts into action. Over time, Moore learned to see her wealth as a tool. "Like many inheritors, I didn't know how to integrate the money with my values and the rest of my life. If I had found that threshold at 21, it would have made a huge difference. But I'm still on the journey of understanding how to use my position of privilege in a positive way."

Giving Away an Inheritance

For others who come into family money, the journey doesn't take quite so long.

Veteran philanthropist Tracy Gary, for instance, has been on a parallel mission to that of Claude Rosenberg—only she began at a much younger age. For years now, Gary has been trying to convince wealthy Americans to increase how much they give.

An offspring of the Pillsbury family, Gary grew up, as she says, with "houses in New York, Florida, Minnesota, Wisconsin and Paris, France." As a youngster, she was ferried about in Rolls-Royces, helicopters, and planes. But at twenty-one, upon taking control of a trust fund inheritance of more than a million dollars, she saw that too many of the wealthy people she knew were far from happy. Their money wasn't buying love or purpose, faith or compassion. Worse, perhaps, she felt the wealth was hamstringing their lives, keeping them isolated and fearful, as it did with Moore. As a result, Gary began giving away her money to causes that worked for social change. By her mid-thirties, she had given away the entire trust fund, launched her career as a donor-activist, and begun donating up to half of her income every year.

How to Determine Your Level of Giving

Today, in her late fifties, Gary runs a Houston-based consultancy for donors, called Inspired Legacies. She recommends approaching the idea of how much to give by first thinking about your values and compassion, rather than your discretionary dollars. "One way to reduce the anxiety about money is to unearth the beliefs you hold about it," she says. This route, in her phrase, often "unleashes generosity."

To sort out the right level for you, as well as the kind of impact you could have, you need to gain an overview of your entire financial picture, assets as well as income. Just be mindful that financial advisors such as investment counselors, trust fund directors, and accountants reflexively recommend contributing a percentage of your annual income. In this lexicon, anything over 5 percent is defined as extraordinarily generous. But such pros are concerned with growing and husbanding your money, not expanding your charitable and personal horizons. "Advisors and estate planners might ask how much you plan to give, but most of them still don't think it's their business to help people go through a process of figuring out how much they can really afford," says Boston-based consultant Christopher Ellinger, who, along with his wife, Anne, works to educate donors on being effective.

How Much Wealth Is Enough?

The Ellingers have been asking that question of donors for years. The answers are still surprising them. Back in the 1980s, the idea of donating principal wealth to charity during your lifetime was considered either outlandish or foolhardy. Few people so much as mentioned it. Yet Anne and Christopher Ellinger chose to defy the convention.

After a double whammy of unexpected inheritances from Christopher's grandparents—roughly $500,000, or about

$1 million in today's dollars—the couple decided they had enough money, thank you very much. So after buying a big house just outside Boston, where they still live, and making investments for their son's education and their future security, they began giving away the bulk of the fortune.

Ultimately, that bold act led the couple into their life's work: founding and running nonprofits that promote philanthropy and the arts. But at the time, in their twenties, and working low-level jobs—she was in social work; he was doing community organizing—the Ellingers wrestled with the weight of sudden wealth. They had several hundred thousand dollars, more than anyone they knew, and no one to talk to about it.

"We knew there was a general rule that you don't give principal, but it didn't make sense to us," recalls Anne. "Part of our thinking was, how much do we really need?" says Christopher.

They decided to seek out people who had actually done it, actually given away their money. "We had to work really hard to find them," says Christopher, because people wouldn't open up about such giving. Still, says Anne, "we thought we should hear their stories before we did something rash. We wanted to see if they regretted it." Instead, the stories were so inspirational that their personal project soon turned into *We Gave Away a Fortune*, a book of personal stories and advice from donors who had contributed anywhere from a few thousand to millions of dollars.

Along the way, the Ellingers realized they weren't alone in wondering how much money it takes to be "rich" or in questioning the taboo against donating chunks of assets while you're still around to appreciate the impact. "We saw people moved to tears, excited to have a place to talk about this where they weren't attacked," says Anne. As a result, the couple conceived More Than Money (MTM), an educational nonprofit that helped people strike a balance between their personal values and their deep pockets. "It wasn't just philanthropy," says Christopher. "More Than Money looked at money values for the whole person." One early MTM supporter was Ruth Ann Harnisch, a former award-winning Nashville journalist and TV news anchor who became wealthy after marrying a successful investment banker. "I got my money the old-fashioned way," says Harnisch. "I earned it, and I married it."

To help people feel in control of their money instead of the other way around, MTM sponsored get-togethers, set up peer-coaching networks, supported giving circles, and published a magazine that explored the personal side of significant wealth, including how to manage the expectations of friends and family.

MTM folded in June 2006, owing to funding and management woes. Its assets and magazines went to the Money and Values Project at the Marpa Center for Business and Economics at Naropa University in Boulder, which continues the work. Harnisch says the organization helped her dispel stereotypical ideas she had about people with money, despite her own wealth. "More Than Money taught me that wealthy people are individuals—surprise!—just like human beings with lesser amounts."

In 2004, the Ellingers launched a new nonprofit, the 50% League, building on ideas that had surfaced at MTM. An audacious philanthropic venture, the league encourages bolder giving by welcoming anyone who makes a one-time donation of at least half their assets or a commitment to donate half or more of their annual income for at least three consecutive years. Members agree to have their stories publicized, anonymously if they choose, and are invited to help promote the league's mission.

But the 50% League is really out to change mindsets, not numbers. "Most people do feel a need to make some sort of contribution," says Christopher. "But while there's a lot of information available about the nuts and bolts of giving and good grant making, there's very little on how to figure out how much to give."

Having wealthy donors who speak publicly about giving half or more of their money to philanthropy as role models translates into smart marketing, according to the Ellingers. It can change the conversation and inspire other givers. "We're unusual," says Ellinger, "but we're not as unusual as people might think. Our goal is to become less and less unusual."

It's Okay to Make Some Mistakes

As a result of the growing interest in the kind of giving that leverages assets and that's fulfilled during a lifetime (rather than as a bequest), a new wave of advisors has sprung up to help donors more carefully assess their capacities. "Donors must have trusted advisors to consider the challenges of the transfer of their wealth," says Gary. You may want to explore some of these avenues (see Chapters 7 and 8) and review some of the alternatives for giving that follow.

Most important, recommends Moore, during the early stages of becoming a donor, allow yourself some experimentation. "People don't take the first steps out of timidity," she says. "They worry about making mistakes, and think they must have a total vision, with all *i*'s dotted and *t*'s crossed before they begin. But the real way to begin donating is to build partnerships with organizations, to make that $500 or $25,000 donation and see how it comes out."

"Don't wait," says Moore.

Volunteering: The News in Hands-on Help

Nonprofits need a range of engaged givers of all stripes to harness new ideas and to connect with and serve diverse constituencies. "I was 20 years old when I started fund-raising," says Tish Hooker Fort, who was married to John Jay Hooker, Jr., Tennessee lawyer and onetime candidate for governor, when she first got involved in philanthropy in the late 1960s. "But now, I think volunteering has become the coin of the realm," she says. "When people volunteer, it helps their soul, it helps socially, it helps business and it helps the community."

Donating time and talent usually involves more of a commitment than giving money does. "Time is the only resource you can't get back," points out Marnie Maxwell, an Indianapolis fund-raising consultant. "You can earn more money, but never more time." So contributing time or skills often represents a greater engagement and more sacrifice than writing checks. Yet volunteers, who have traditionally tended to be women, rarely command the attention or respect generated by megadonors, who have typically been men.

That's not to suggest donors of dollars don't also roll up their sleeves. Increasingly, most do. But the tradition of volunteering has long been undervalued and discounted. There's still that myth out there that volunteers are the ladies who lunch; that is, groups of affluent women searching for something to occupy their days.

Yet recent research by David Reingold, a professor at the University of Indiana's School of Public and Environmental Affairs, reveals just the opposite. "The more women work, the more likely they are to volunteer," says Reingold. "The gender differences that have been so present during the twentieth century really are coming to an end. The stereotypical image of volunteering as a substitute for working by stay-at-home moms or retired grandmothers is simply not true anymore."

Nationwide, Who
Volunteers What

In 2007, nearly 61 million adults volunteered their time, giving more than 8 billion hours of service, worth about $158 billion, according to the Corporation for National and Community Service, a federal agency that tracks data and oversees AmeriCorps and Senior Corps. In addition, from 2006 to 2007, more than a third of those volunteers served a hundred hours or more, an annual jump of almost 375,000 in so-called intensive volunteers.

Nonetheless, an ongoing challenge is the growing dropout rate for first-time volunteers, or what the service calls "the leaky bucket." More than one out of every three Americans in the past few years—an estimated 22 million— try volunteering but soon stop. Those numbers, according to the agency's most recent report, show "how important it is for organizations that use volunteers to treat them as valuable assets, give them meaningful assignments, and use best practices in volunteer management." In other words, nonprofits aren't tapping volunteer talent as well as they could or should. Conversely, volunteers may not be educated or up-front about what they expect.

Giving Is About More
Than Dollars

These days, both women and men volunteers are likely to be executives, doctors, or—like Almeta Cooper, who works as

National Snapshot of Volunteering, 2007

- ◆ Number of volunteers nationwide: nearly 61 million.
- ◆ National volunteer rate: 27 percent.
- ◆ Total volunteer hours per year: more than 8 billion.
- ◆ Value of volunteer time per year: $158 billion.
- ◆ No. 1 region: Midwest, at 32 percent.
- ◆ No. 1 state: Utah, at nearly 44 percent.
- ◆ No. 1 large city: Minneapolis–St. Paul, at just more than 39 percent.
- ◆ Intensive volunteering is on the rise: The percentage of volunteers giving over 100 hours of service per year reached 36 percent, its highest level since 2002.
- ◆ College towns are hot spots, reflecting the correlation between higher levels of education and volunteering.
- ◆ Women volunteer more than men, and working mothers have the highest rate: About 29 percent of women volunteered in 2007, compared to 23 percent of men. Women with children and women who work have higher volunteer rates than other women.

"Volunteering in America: 2008 State and City Trends & Rankings," Corporation for National and Community Service

general counsel for the Ohio State Medical Association in Columbus—lawyers. "It was my daughter who got me interested in volunteering in 2002," says Cooper. Then in her first year of high school (and now a Bryn Mawr graduate), Elise Nelson was invited to participate in a project designed to introduce girls to philanthropy through working with the YWCA and other groups.

"They toured some programs, got involved in grant writing and conducted interviews with grantees—it was very exciting for them," says Cooper, who divorced when Elise was five. "It was a valuable experience for her, and I've since volunteered several times in fund-raising campaigns, as a grants reader and other activities," she says.

After her daughter left for college, Cooper became more engaged, mostly with the Women's Fund of Central Ohio and also with the local chapter of the Links, an international group of professional African American women volunteers who work for social change. "I never turn down a request from the Women's Fund," says Cooper, "because they train people to have an effective, structured plan and they give women and girls a voice."

What to Know Before You Volunteer

Volunteering isn't only about giving, either. It's also about getting something back. "You don't have to be purely altruistic to volunteer," says Lynn Korda Kroll, who would know. Her résumé includes some thirty years of volunteering, from stints at her local library when her four kids were young to her current board and policy work at the UJA (United Jewish Appeal)-Federation, which, in 2007, raised $290 million. "Volunteering has been my career and I take it seriously," says Kroll, whose husband Jules founded Kroll, Inc., the security- and risk-management consultancy. "But

Ten Tips for Trouble-Free Volunteering

The following tips were developed by Independent Sector, a nonprofit membership coalition of charities and corporate-giving programs. When you volunteer, keep them in mind.

1. Choose causes or issues you feel strongly about.

2. Decide whether you want an opportunity to be trained or to learn new skills.

3. Make sure your commitment is serious enough to sustain consistent and long-term help.

4. Identify the skills you can offer.

5. Consider including friends or family.

6. Expect to be interviewed; nonprofits have requirements, too.

7. Remember virtual volunteering, such as phone or online advice, work, or support.

8. Create your own opportunity by forming a group to offer what you want.

9. Don't wait to be asked.

10. Be patient. If your first choice isn't a good fit for you, try another.

volunteering is also about making new friends, learning new skills and finding a community of like-minded people."

When considering a volunteer role, be prepared to pay some dues, advises Abby Disney, who first got involved in philanthropy by volunteering at a few New York City social services agencies. "I volunteered because I wanted to hold the babies," she says. But she soon realized she had to earn that privilege by first doing other chores. "As a volunteer, you can't say you just want to do certain things. Instead, just show up and say, 'Use me.'"

Keep in mind that organizations bank on your commitment. When you do volunteer, avoid making promises you won't have time to keep. Saying no is preferable to saying maybe. In addition, make sure you find a good match, both in the cause and in the spirit and activities of the nonprofit. As with contributing money, don't volunteer simply because your friends are doing so. Make sure you can consistently show up over the long term, and give yourself the freedom to review the options before you commit. "Because if you make a snap judgment," says consultant Maxwell, "you're liable to find yourself at a meeting wondering why you're wasting your most valuable resource, your time."

When You're Ready for a Heartfelt Getaway

Volunteer vacations are proliferating. About 40 percent of Americans say they're willing to spend several weeks away on vacations that involve volunteer service, with another 13 percent wanting to spend an entire year, according to an April 2008 survey by the University of California, San Diego. Socially responsible vacation programs now provide treks and trips for every taste, from saving animals and restoring historic landmarks to constructing schools and joining archeological digs. Three major groups that arrange such vacations are the American Hiking Society (which helps restore and maintain national and state parks), the Sierra Club (which focuses on environmental projects) and Habitat for Humanity (which helps build low-cost housing). The most diverse programs are probably offered by Earthwatch, which sets up trips for volunteers to accompany a scientist on a research expedition. Also check out CrossCulturalSolutions.org, GlobalVolunteers.org, and VolunTourism.org for more choices.

Just remember that you're usually required to pay a hefty fee for the privilege of going on these trips. Still, most travelers feel it's worth the adventure and the contribution to the cause.

Beyond Check-Writing: Creative Ways to Give

There are dozens of other options for giving besides writing a check or volunteering time. Gifts of financial securities and real estate tend to be the most popular. Recently, the IRS began releasing the value of noncash charitable gifts that taxpayers report on their itemized returns. Its latest study, released in 2007, found that more than 25 million taxpayers who itemized deductions had donated more than $41 billion worth of noncash property in charitable contributions—up 11 percent from the $37 billion donated in tax year 2004.

Before taking any such action, however, check with your tax and financial advisors.

Ideas You May Not Have Thought About

♦ Give your house. Gifts of real estate cover a wide variety of choices—houses, apartment buildings, farms, vacation homes, commercial buildings, and both income-producing and non-income-producing land—says Mary Ellis Peterson, gift-planning officer at the Minneapolis Foundation. "You can cede your mortgage to the foundation and, when it's paid up, continue to live in the home for the rest of your life." Upon your death, the house passes to any charity you select. The nonprofit can then sell it and use the proceeds. "One couple, who were missionaries, gave their house to a community foundation, and after their death, the money from the home has continued to support their missions around the world," says Peterson. A gift of real estate that you've owned for more than a year entitles you to a tax deduction for the full fair market value of the property, while still allowing you to avoid capital gains tax. Typically, gifts of real estate require a series of steps, including a property-site visit, a qualified appraisal, a title report, and an environmental assessment. As a result, such gifts can raise complex tax and legal issues. Fortunately, most public foundations or charities have planned-giving experts, like Peterson, who'd be delighted to help you work through the process.

♦ Give by the dozen. The vast majority of people who give to charity wait until December to make donations, partly because of the holiday spirit and usually in order to qualify for that year's tax deductions. But you can rate the same annual tax break by giving in January or June. And with monthly donations, you create a habit and ease cash flow. "I usually give about $12,000 to charity at the end of the year," says lawyer Miriam Buhl, who directs the pro bono program at New York law firm Weil, Gotshal & Manges. "But I've decided to plan my giving and donate the equivalent of $1,000 a month—it'll make it a lot easier."

♦ Create a gift registry. A number of online offerings, including the well-known I Do Foundation (idofoundation.org), allow you to set up a personal channel to invite family, friends, and associates to make gifts to a charity to commemorate events like weddings, anniversaries, birthdays, and graduations. Just be careful to vet the site beforehand. Make sure, first, that it's a legitimate business and, next, that the lion's share of the gift goes to your charity of choice (see Chapter 5 for how to evaluate a charitable organization).

♦ Give the rewards of intellectual property. If you've written a book or screenplay, or own a patent, donate a percentage of incoming royalties or fees. A few years ago, playwright Carol Mack heard about the work of Vital Voices Global

Partnership, which supports women community leaders around the world. Mack was motivated to organize a project with six other women playwrights, who all donated their work. Called *Seven,* their play dramatizes the lives of seven women supported by Vital Voices who are fighting the odds and the cultures in places like Russia, where one is working to expose the domestic abuse that kills 14,000 women a year; Afghanistan, where a midwife defied the Taliban; and Pakistan, where a young woman named Mukhtaran Mai, was honor gang-raped but still brought her attackers to justice. A male tribunal in Mai's village sentenced her to be raped by four men as punishment, because her twelve-year-old brother had supposedly held hands with a girl from a higher-caste tribe. Instead of committing suicide after the rape, which tradition dictated in order to restore honor to her family, Mai challenged the legal system and brought suit against the men—and won. She used the payment she received in damages to build a school for girls.

A percentage of *Seven*'s royalties now goes to Vital Voices. "I gave up a year of my own work to do this," says Mack, who contributed a piece about Inez McCormack, a Protestant Irish trade unionist, to the play. "I thought if we illuminated their lives this way onstage, it might help to call attention to them."

- ♦ Give a matching gift. Check to see if your company will match the gift you make to a nonprofit group or will make a grant based on your recommendation.

- Give used items. But remember that things you value aren't necessarily so to a nonprofit. When donating used items, such as clothing or furnishings, find out whether it's truly useful to the charity—call and ask. You will also need to get a receipt of acknowledgment in order to rate a tax deduction. Many charities sell donated items to other groups to raise cash. If the idea of turning your gift into cash bothers you—say, that winter coat you thought would clothe a needy individual—ask about the policies. Such sales also can influence your tax deduction.

- Give collaboratively. Set up a giving circle with friends, family, or colleagues to leverage your dollars and impact. These easygoing groups forge their own rules and choices, often with back-office help from a community or public foundation. If your pals live across town or are scattered around the world, consider a virtual circle. Use free online tools like Skype, Microsoft Office Live Meeting, or instant messaging to electronically collaborate in real time. (See Chapter 6 for more on giving circles.)

- Give art, antiques, or collectibles. Like a house, these gifts can be donated to a qualified charity and still remain in your possession during your lifetime. The gift goes to the nonprofit after you die. But check with financial pros beforehand. Such gifts have become more complicated and less of a tax break in recent years, owing to changes mandated by Congress in 2006. (See Chapter 7 for more on taxes and charitable gifts.)

- Give with a legacy. By setting up a charitable remainder trust (CRT) with cash assets or stock, you live on the trust's income during your lifetime, while the principal passes to a qualified charity after you die. Just remember that CRTs are irrevocable—you can't change one after it's established. You can also contribute retirement plan assets, such as 401(k) accounts and IRAs (see Chapter 10).

- Give technology. More and more groups, online and off, provide recycling outlets to donate used cell phones, PDAs, computers, peripherals, software, and the like. For opportunities and guidelines, check with local community foundations, public schools, small-business training centers, or sites like UniversalGiving.org and ShareTechnology.org. One online organization, Secure the Call Foundation (donatemycellphone.org), estimates that there are over 45 million old cell phones sitting in drawers and closets. Any mobile phone that can be turned on can be used for free emergency calls. Nonprofits can convert these to 911 emergency-use mobiles and give them to, say, women suffering from domestic abuse and kids at risk. Don't forget to delete personal information and wipe hard drives clean of data before making such gifts.

- Give mutual fund shares or appreciated securities. Besides netting a potentially significant tax savings (up to 30 percent of your adjusted gross income) and an immediate charitable deduction for the market value of the donated assets, giving mutual fund shares that transfer to a qualified charity after you die will exempt you from any capital gains tax on the appreciation. Once again, check with your financial advisors before proceeding.

♦ Give a car. When donating a vehicle, keep in mind that it's the donor, not the nonprofit, who values the car for the purposes of a tax deduction. You therefore need to be clear about its worth. Take and retain photos, and save receipts for any new parts, tires, or the like.

♦ Give part of your business. If you own limited partnership interests (rather than stock in a private family business), you can contribute these to a qualifying charity. Again, this can get complicated, so be prepared to plan carefully.

♦ Give a platform. Lisa Ling, who's in her mid-thirties, is a TV correspondent for both the National Geographic Channel and the *Oprah Winfrey Show*. She travels widely in the developing world and "is exposed to very challenging stories that often pertain to women and children, especially because Oprah's objective is to cover stories that don't get a lot of attention." Ling also speaks at universities and to women's groups to raise awareness and money. Early in 2008, she launched an interactive blog that's part news resource and part call to action. You might try something similar. "I want to raise consciousness about issues and stories that don't always make the headlines," says Ling.

♦ Give to a social venture investment fund. Several non-profit investment companies around the country work for change by lending money at very low interest rates. When you invest money, you get a return, which will vary by project and firm. For example, Elyse Cherry, a real estate

Guide to Donating Noncash Gifts

Here's a three-step plan for maximizing the impact of noncash donations, developed by Charity Navigator, an online nonprofit that rates the nation's largest charities for efficiency and performance.

1. Determine whether the items you wish to donate are useful. Most charities can only make use of items that are new, unused, or nearly new. If you don't have any use for your old, tattered couch; rusty washing machine; or other used item, chances are neither will a charity.

2. Consider selling your items and donating the proceeds to charity. By donating cash instead of goods you allow charities greater flexibility in spending the money so that it reaches those who need it the most. And by selling the items yourself, you'll know the exact value of the donation to report to the IRS and won't have to estimate it for tax returns.

3. Find a nearby charity. In order to avoid transportation costs, which can lessen the impact of your donation, look first in your local community to find a charity to support with your noncash contribution. Call around and ask charities if they accept the kind of items you are looking to donate, and, if not, ask for suggestions.

lawyer, runs Boston Community Capital, a social venture capital fund that has roughly $300 million assets under management, up from only $10 million a decade ago. Her fund has built charter schools, health clinics, affordable housing, child-care facilities, and more. "We've made $308 million in loans," says Cherry, "and over ten years only lost $108,000." And in New York City's Harlem, Sheena Wright runs Abyssinian Development Corporation and is similarly revitalizing the community.

♦ Give your life insurance policy. "A life insurance policy is an ideal tool for charitable giving, because many people find they no longer need policies they purchased earlier in their lifetimes," says the Minneapolis Foundation's Mary Ellis Peterson. Basically, you assign the policy to the charity (while still covering the annual premiums) and make the charity the beneficiary. If the policy is paid up, you receive an immediate tax deduction equal to the policy's cash value at the time.

Chapter 5

HOW CAN YOU CHECK OUT A CHARITY?

MAKING YOUR MONEY WORK

The frontier for nonprofits these days is *impact*. How do you measure the social good you do? For that matter, how do you measure which cultural arts are worthwhile or what kind of educational efforts will be effective a decade down the road? What does *success* mean in the charitable arena?

Lately, forward-looking practitioners are walking away from trying to define or measure impact, mostly because such a goal is so big and amorphous that it's impossible to realize. Donors and charities can't really measure it. As one research group puts it, "How do you prove impact?"

Instead, as donors continue to demand greater roles and results, nonprofits are increasingly focusing on *outcomes* as signs of success. That is, do grantees and groups achieve the stated goals of the funding? While that's still not easy to calculate, at least it's visible and tangible. Such measurement allows for progress.

But then a corollary challenge arises that's equally thorny. Let's say you do quantify the *outcome*—which is now becoming a proxy for *impact*. Then how do you best demonstrate those results to donors and the larger community in order to build awareness, boost contributions, and ensure continuing progress?

"Philanthropy is a tough transition for people who have made money in the business environment and are used to performance measures on a quarterly or daily basis," says Phil Buchanan, president of the Center for Effective Philanthropy in Boston, which works with nonprofit organizations to increase impact. "Donors need to be realistic. Even the largest donors in the world must be conscious of what you can achieve given the resources you have. If you really want to feel and see results of giving, you need to stay pretty focused. It's very hard to do."

Trying to Make Headway Against the Effects of Autism

For example, in 2005, Suzanne Wright and husband Bob, then vice-chairman of General Electric and former CEO of NBC Universal, established the foundation Autism Speaks, because their grandson was diagnosed with the disorder the previous year. Autism now affects 1 in 150 individuals in the United States, according to the U.S. Centers for Disease

Control and Prevention, more than ten times the number of a decade ago.

Helpless against autism's effects on their family, the Wrights decided to leverage their considerable resources and media influence to build awareness and fund research for a cure. Yet even given the couple's high profile and their professional staff, says Suzanne, "running a foundation has given us a new perspective on giving. We understand, more than ever, the challenges of operating an effective and efficient not-for-profit that donors can be confident is spending their money wisely."

Focus on Results, Not Financial Ratios

A conventional rule of thumb for measuring a nonprofit organization's effectiveness is to compare its operating and administrative costs to its spending on programs. When operating costs top 40 percent of the annual budget—which puts spending on programs at 60 percent—it may be an inefficient organization, or something may be wrong. Yet experts repeatedly caution donors not to rely exclusively on such ratios when making decisions about what to fund or judging whether your gift has fueled results.

Charities raise money and carry out programs in widely

different ways, depending on the type of the cause, the organization's location, age and "hip quotient," as well as other factors, according to Charity Navigator. There is no ideal fund-raising percentage or standard for administrative costs that can be applied across the board. In addition, accounting rules allow nonprofits several different methods of calculating fund-raising percentages, which means you may not be comparing apples to apples when you look at such figures.

Then, too, there's plain common sense. Basing your giving decisions entirely on such formulas begs the reality of trying to get the job done. New York donor-activist Barbara Dobkin, whose investment-banker husband, Eric, created

What to Ask a Nonprofit Before Writing a Check

Bob Ottenhof directs GuideStar, a nonprofit donor resource based in Williamsburg, Virginia, that offers free online access to a database of the tax returns or Form 990s filed by more than 1.7 million organizations. He suggests that you ask the following questions of any organization you might consider funding. If you're not satisfied with the answers, think twice before becoming involved.

◆ Are you willing to share audited financial statements?
◆ Who is on your board?
◆ Who is your senior management? What kind of experience do they have, and what is their compensation?
◆ How do you allocate your resources?
◆ Where do you get your money?

the family fortune, contributed about $6 million in stock and outright grants in 2006, including her usual annual support for the White House Project. A decade ago, Dobkin donated $1 million to help launch the project, which works to put women into top electoral and corner offices. Her support of causes and programs extends to organizations. "I also fund operating costs," she says, "because if an organization can't pay its staff and turn on the lights and have an office, how do you expect them to be successful with programs?"

When you are thinking about a donation or a contribution of any kind, the best measure of an organization's impact is how efficiently and effectively it is fulfilling its mission.

How Doris Buffett Learned to Be Effective

That doesn't mean you shouldn't expect *accountability*—the sector's current buzzword for a range of organizational behaviors, from sharing information to being true to the mission to harnessing dollars and resources efficiently. But most donors need some time to learn how to set appropriate benchmarks for grantees or organizations. That was certainly the case for Doris Buffett.

"I believe in a hand up rather than a handout," she says, summing up her activist approach with characteristic simplicity. "I'm turned off by the image of a lady with a lot of money doling things out of her basket."

Now in her early eighties, Buffett got serious about

philanthropy only after her mother died in 1996 and she came into what she calls "the big money"—a trust with considerable shares in Berkshire Hathaway. That, of course, is the famously successful holding company controlled by her equally famous younger brother Warren, no slouch at philanthropy himself. Doris shares the trust—worth maybe $300 million—with a sister. A child of the Depression like her legendary brother, she shares his deep thriftiness.

For a few years before the inheritance, Warren gave Doris control of about $100,000 a year, through one of his children's small foundations. She made grants and learned the ropes. "I was living in a small town on the North Carolina coast, in a very poor area," says Buffett. "I got a big bang for the buck." She also learned from her mistakes. "You can want something for someone more than they want it themselves. I would see ways to fix things and move in. But I learned you have to collaborate."

Nowadays, Buffett runs her own busy nonprofit, the Sunshine Lady Foundation, with a minimal, all-women staff, a grandson on the board, and two areas of dedicated interest. First, the foundation works to break "cycles of poverty, abuse and economic dependence, through investment in education. Women, especially those who experience domestic violence, and children always come first." Second, it works to encourage philanthropy, mostly by setting an example in funding schools and students.

Among other efforts, Buffett has sponsored reading programs, staved off foreclosures, provided practical help for women escaping violence, created a community orthodontics program, repaired roofs, and built home additions. She also teaches a course as a visiting professor at several colleges called—what else?—Philanthropy 101. And she has began supporting girls and women in Afghanistan—"I know I'm taking a chance, because I usually nail down the problem in this country, but I became impassioned." In 2007, Buffett spent $10 million in grants. Her goal for the next few years is $1 million a month.

Early on, to find the right matches and organizations, she recruited help from about a hundred friends, family, and associates around the country—"adjunct program directors" in nonprofit parlance, but "Sunbeams" in Buffett's vocabulary. These helpers earn fees, with a ceiling of $10,000 each a year, by sending her one-page site reports about needs and opportunities in their communities. "Giving away money is no easy task, if it's done responsibly and effectively, and there's no good reason to try to do it alone," she says. "We get value for every dollar we spend." Now, with so many programs up and going, the number of participating Sunbeams has dropped to sixty or so.

Buffett requires every grantee to sign an agreement that spells out specific expectations—and she enforces it. "I stop funding them if they break the contract," she says. Even the eight-year-olds she sends to summer camp—"the best camps in North Carolina"—must earn their way. They promise to obey their parents, do well in school, and "do kind things for other people." Generally, she says, "I try to follow sensible things where there's cause and effect, like a business, but with a big heart."

Buffett also typically leverages her dollars with challenge or matching grants and, really, just by asking people in need to do more to help themselves before she'll respond. Not long ago, for instance, she was forwarded a letter from the local newspaper, which had featured a story about her, from a woman in trouble. "Hattie Lou said her house was tumbling down, her furniture was broken and she couldn't work as a nurse anymore because of her arthritis. I checked it out and it was true. She was a wonderful worker and had to stop because of arthritis." So Buffett wrote back, asking if anyone else was living in the house. She learned about an unemployed husband who had quit a delivery job because he didn't like his route. Buffett's next move? If the husband got a job and sent her a copy of the paycheck, she promised to match it. He had a job within a month. "I like to empower, not enable," she explains.

Fund-Raisers Are Pulling Out All the Stops

As nonprofits multiply and more people at every income level become involved, the competition for charitable dollars has turned fierce. In turn, fund-raising is getting both more innovative and, in some instances, unscrupulous.

On the one hand, a lot of fund-raising is now admirably inventive and considerably disciplined. The sector is cautiously learning how to market itself and engage with donors of different races, classes, genders, and ethnic backgrounds.

Organizations are also working to put excitement into fund-raising benefits, spirit into 10K races, and sizzle into charity auctions. In Chicago, for instance, Maureen Smith, wife of banking scion E. B. Smith, has been the prime mover in getting the Joffrey Ballet back on pointe after it ran out of funds and relocated from New York to the Windy City in 1995.

A dedicated philanthropist and devoted dance aficionado, Smith relies on a range of methods and events to raise badly needed funds for the Joffrey. She has formed a powerful board of fifteen or so influential women who network with friends and colleagues not only for donations but also for ideas and resources. "We announced a campaign for $35 million, but first we raised $17.5 million of that," she says. "That gave us credibility."

Smith has boosted awareness for the troupe by organizing free, festive outdoor performances. That's led to alliances with the City, and to recruiting Mayor Daley to attend the Joffrey's fiftieth anniversary party, attended by a crowd of 10,000, at Millennium Park in 2006. "It mattered that we could have a photo op with the mayor and his wife," says Smith. "It was picked up by the press and was a tremendous success."

Similarly, across the country in recent years, board members, volunteers, and staff development officers have been dreaming up dozens of creative events and forums to draw interest, participants, and a stream of steady donations.

On the other hand, today's fund–raising has its excesses. Despite the legitimacy of thousands of groups, the ethics of some major nonprofits have come under scrutiny because certain organizations misused donations outright or diverted funds questionably. "Many of the scams were ones that did not just take advantage of individual donors but of all of us as citizens, because they had to do with taxes," says Bob Ottenhof, president of GuideStar. "That undermines the confidence and trust that individuals have in nonprofits." Other organizations deliberately adopt names similar to larger, well-known groups in order to trade on donor confusion and tug at your heartstrings. Still others spend most of their money on telemarketing or TV appeals rather than on the programs they're so busy peddling.

As a result, several groups in the field have developed a code of ethics, a donor bill of rights, if you will. Based in

The Fed Is on Your Side

It's just become easier to track where a charity's money goes and how much it spends on programs, expenses, salaries, administrative costs, and so on. For the first time in twenty years, the IRS, which regulates nonprofits, has redesigned Form 990, or the tax form that charities and other tax-exempt organizations file each year. The new form, which charities must make available upon request, takes effect as of tax year 2008, which means 2009 filings. Changes include the following:

- ♦ a top-page summary that compares revenue and expenses over a two-year period;
- ♦ a page that requires charities to list all of their accomplishments over the past year;
- ♦ new sections that require more detailed information about fundraising, governance, and compensation for trustees and executives.

Washington, D.C., Independent Sector, a nonprofit advocacy coalition of about 600 organizations, recommends to its members that donors have the right to know the name of anyone soliciting contributions; the name and location of the organization receiving contributions; the intended use of the funds; whether the individual soliciting is a volunteer, an organization employee, or hired help; and more.

Generally, if you're asked for a donation and you cannot learn exactly who's asking or details about where the money is going, you should probably walk away.

"Take giving as seriously as you do investing," says Trent Stamp, who founded and ran watchdog group Charity Navigator from 2001 to 2007, and who is currently executive director of the Eisner Foundation. "The biggest mistake people make is being reactive." Instead, he suggests, "Get out in front of your choices, decide what you want to fund and vet the group you're considering to see if their goals align with yours over the long term."

Plan B for Poverty

"People underestimate the time and energy it takes to bring about the kind of change we're trying to bring," says Geoffrey Canada, chief executive of the Harlem Children's Zone (HCZ), in New York City.

An ambitious experiment, HCZ began in 1997 by targeting a twenty-four-block area of central Harlem and providing comprehensive kindergarten-through-college services, including education, family care, medical help, psychological and social support, and after-school training—in other words, year-round cradle-to-college remedies. The program has since expanded to a hundred-block area and now has assets of more than $109 million.

Success has generated substantial national attention for HCZ, most recently from President Barack Obama, who, during his campaign, promised to replicate Canada's HCZ model in twenty cities across the country. But however worthy, the Harlem Children's Zone Project isn't making headlines because of its cause. Programs to help poor kids in troubled communities have been around forever. Rather, it's the way HCZ goes about its work that attracts the spotlight. "The main things that separate us from similar organizations is that we have a clear strategic plan and we are focused on outcomes," says Canada.

Geoffrey Canada grew up hard in the violent South Bronx and found his way out via a scholarship to Maine's Bowdoin College and a Harvard graduate degree in education. Now in his mid-fifties, and after two decades of working with kids in tough settings, Canada is a persuasive veteran of the failed wars on poverty. HCZ is his plan B.

Working against a detailed strategic plan developed in 2001 that helped to draw $46 million in initial backing, HCZ offers an energizing redefinition of the goal of supporting at-risk children. "In the last twenty-five years, children have been failing by the hundreds in communities like South Central Los Angeles, Bedford-Stuyvesant, and Harlem, because we haven't defined what winning is," says Canada. The first issue he points to is the emphasis on funding early childhood and after-school programs. "It's wasted a lot of money because people haven't thought through what it means to take a child to the finish line— and the finish line is college," he says.

"The second issue is scale," he continues. "There are over a million kids in the New York school system and about 250,000 are failing. Programs that have celebrated success have only had a couple hundred kids."

By contrast, in 2006, the HCZ Project served more than 10,500 individuals, including nearly 6,900 kids, and the programs continue to expand. The project is expected to serve more than 10,000 at-risk children over the next few years. Trying to change the odds takes smart planning, as well as time and money. "We work with kids from 8:00 a.m. to 6:00 p.m.," says Canada. "It's about growth strategy and accountability."

Making Your Contributions Count

Before funding any organization, investigate its background. Research its past performance, progress, and grant-making history so that you can ask informed questions or resolve any issues when you meet with the fund-raiser or development officer. Virtually all nonprofit organizations and advocacy groups now host Web sites, which means you can learn a great deal about a group online before setting up a meeting. Talk to some board members, grantees, and donors, many of whom are also listed on the sites.

You'll want to look into the group's financials. Do check whether your donation is tax deductible, which tells you that the group has been designated as a legitimate nonprofit. Request its annual report or check its annual Form 990 tax filing. Be wary of any group unfamiliar to you that asks for credit card contributions over the phone, pressures you to donate, or requests personal information in a door-to-door request. These could be scams. Don't give cash to anyone you don't know, either.

Ask how the organization uses donors' personal information. Do they, for instance, sell donor lists to other charity telemarketers or direct mail campaigns? Can they honor your request for anonymity, should you prefer that? Is the online contribution channel for the charity encrypted and safe?

Build a Relationship with Nonprofits That Will Get You Results

Increasingly, as donors accompany their financial backing with hands-on involvement, they are joining forces with the organizations they support in order to leverage contributions and advance the mission. Like any relationship, though, establishing an honest, effective donor-charity alliance built on trust and understanding takes time and compromise.

While the third sector is clearly trying harder these days to be both donor-friendly and more transparent, such partnerships still often throw up tensions. Usually, the strain stems from misunderstanding the other side's motivations.

Since nonprofits depend on contributions and grants, development officers and fund-raisers may wax poetic when describing their programs and outcomes and may gloss over some real challenges and difficulties. Unsurprisingly, this can offend donors, who may know better. Or, the cheery overview may cause donors to feel that the organization is less than competent or, worse, hiding something. No one wins in such circumstances, and, thankfully, such happy talk is fading from the field.

More frequently these days, charities simply cannot command the specific details that directly address donor questions. "Many nonprofits, even the largest, established institutions, don't define goals," says the Center for Effective Philanthropy's Phil Buchanan. "Choosing goals is tied up with assessing results, so the organization must figure out what's working and what's not. But there's no common unit of measurement for charitable impact, no analog for the business world's ROI. You also have to measure the impact you're having relative to the resources you have, which means weighing social good versus grants out the door. Across different programs and goals, it's not possible to boil down to a single number. Another challenge is causality: If an organization is funding 4 percent or 5 percent or 6 percent of a project or mission, what is the connection between when you fund and what happened on the ground?"

How, indeed, do you convey this complex picture to expectant donors who are considering a contribution of $1,000 or $1 million depending on whether the nonprofit can adequately explain how the money will be spent and the precise result it will fund? The answer is that it takes a lot of goodwill and honest conversation—as well as ongoing donor education.

On the other side, once the check is cashed, donors sometimes turn intrusive or overbearing, feeling they've bought the right to express their opinions and direct decisions. And they certainly should have a voice. But many donors don't take the time to become knowledgeable before weighing in. They may not bother to tap the nonprofit's expertise in identifying where or how they can be most useful. Before wading in, make sure you know as much as you can.

There's also the troublesome challenge of novelty. Entrenched, familiar social problems aren't nearly as interesting as fresh, trendy ones. "Donors like to support new ideas and innovations," says Diana Aviv, chief executive of Independent Sector. "But the proliferation of nonprofit organizations is not sustainable. Nonprofits can't always respond to a culture of donors that wants new things. There isn't sufficient funding. Organizations will end up spending more time on fund-raising than on delivering on their programs. We need

DEFINING THE CHALLENGE

"In order to wrap money around problems, you first need to get the problem right. These days, a greater number of people are trying to ask that question, not how much are we giving and not how magnanimous are we, but how much are we accomplishing? That's the real question."
—SUSAN RAYMOND, CHANGING OUR WORLD

to define support so organizations can succeed in profound and meaningful ways that change conditions."

How to Drive the Learning Curve in Making Successful Grants

In the mid-nineties, Patricia Gruber was a psychotherapist with a thriving practice in Berkeley, California. She felt that she made a difference. "I had a great referral network and a lot of support from local people in the field." But her husband, Peter, an investment manager with clients that included the late billionaire mutual fund founder Sir John Templeton, was offered a job in St. Thomas, in the U.S. Virgin Islands. They decided to move. "It was a big transition," says Gruber. "I felt like I was too far along in my career to start over."

Then her father became ill, and she spent the next three years devoted to his care. In 2000, after her father died, Gruber gradually got involved with the private foundation that her husband had been operating on his own—"he made all the money, and the foundation was his idea," she explains.

Life took a turn. "It developed a whole other side of me. I did not have an MBA or any nonprofit management experience, and I never thought I'd be suited for it, or that it would make me feel so happy and capable," she says.

To get up to speed, Gruber took an online course in grant

making offered by the Council on Foundations, a nonprofit membership association. "I learned the basic protocols, which dovetailed with my background in social services." She also set up learning sessions with other foundation

Sample Forms to Manage Grant Requests and Site Visits

After tapping the experience of a few consultants and other foundation owners, Gruber developed these two simple but effective forms to streamline the process of (1) filtering requests for funding and (2) assessing a project or grantee during a site visit.

Donation Request

Dear _____,

Thank you for your request for financial support from _____ (FOUNDATION NAME), which we received on _____ (DATE).

We make every effort to respond quickly, usually within a two-week time frame. However, to fully consider this request, we need more information. Can you please provide the following items marked with a check mark:

__ A copy of documentation showing your group's status as a tax-exempt, nonprofit organization (501[c][3] status).

__ A copy of the organization's most recent budget, including staff costs, which will be held in confidence.

___ An outline of specifically how the donation would be spent, including how many individuals will be served by the organization; the amount of money needed for specific items.

If you have any questions, please feel free to call me at
_____ .

We look forward to hearing from you.

Sincerely,

_____

Site Visit Report Form

Date of site visit:

Visited by:

Name of program and date established:

General purpose:

501(c)(3) letter on file:

Program staff:

Population served:

Cost of services to population:

Code of ethics or ethical guidelines:

General funding source(s):

Other fund-raising activities:

Approximate annual budget:

Description of facility:

Pertinent input from staff and/or population served:

Successes/shortcomings and general comments:

owners, worked with consultants, and tagged along on some field visits, including, says Gruber, an inspiring and enlightening trip with global financier and philanthropist George Soros to a remote part of Hungary, where he was then funding a school for girls.

The couple always had in mind a mission of rewarding excellence and encouraging research. So rather than making grants, the Peter and Patricia Gruber Foundation awards unrestricted cash prizes of $500,000 each to young scientists in fields such as cosmology, genetics, and neuroscience—"areas the Nobels don't fund," says Gruber. To stay sharp, the foundation, with its roughly $104 million in assets, partners with top-level scientific societies and relies on a panel of international advisors.

The Grubers also award prizes for social justice and women's rights, sometimes combining their two interests. "There have been only about a dozen women who've won science Nobels," says Gruber. Working to change that ratio, the foundation funds a career-development award of $75,000, over three years, to a young woman geneticist from anywhere in the world. "The perception of the scientific community is that there's no big cadre of women marching forward," says Gruber. Yet judges at the American Society of Human Genetics, which administers the award, were floored by the response. "They received more than 200 applications from highly qualified young women for the one position. They had no idea there were so many gifted women out there."

For Pat Gruber, life continues to change.

When Considering Funding, Push Out the Horizon

Consistent funding over several years is the most effective way to fuel results. Organizations work best when they can develop a long-term program and bank on funding it for some years. That allows strategic thinking and action as well as full-time focus on building a successful program. Giving five dollars here and a dollar there certainly helps to solve immediate and compelling needs, but it won't resolve embedded issues.

"Donors and funders who come and go after one to three years generally do good, but they do not sustain organizations and leaders," says philanthropist Tracy Gary. "Assist organizations over long-term funding, say three to five years, and you will see them fly and learn more than you can imagine. This is what donors and nonprofits need to grow and strengthen our sector.

"I have remained a funder of 60 percent of the grants or gifts I make for over seven years. Some for twenty-five years," says Gary.

Putting Restrictions on Your Gift: Pros and Cons

The idea of attaching conditions to gifts as a way to command results is as old as grant making itself. But legendary philanthropist and industrial baron John D. Rockefeller is often credited with bringing the practice to a whole new level of effective leveraging. Over his forty or so years of truly spectacular giving, Rockefeller evolved a system by which he agreed to fund part of a project only if and when grantees secured financial pledges from other donors as well. That was how Rockefeller came to help found the prestigious University of Chicago in 1890, as well as dozens of other educational institutions. For two subsequent decades, Rockefeller continued a steady stream of contributions to the university, but always with the proviso that others share in its support.

As a result of several colliding factors—including the increasing complexity of giving, the proliferation of nonprofits, deeper levels of donor interest, and the spate of well-publicized charity scandals—this traditional idea of making contributions with strings attached has lately attracted many more donors. Usually, this means that at the time they donate, and for gifts of any size or duration, donors specify in a written agreement the exact program, building, research equipment, kind of supplies, social services, or what have you that they want the money to be spent on. The organization must then heed those wishes—or forfeit the contribution.

Such restrictions can offer clear advantages, as is evident from Rockefeller's storied success. Conditional grants do ensure that your money will be spent just as you wish and on nothing else. But today, donor restrictions are growing both more numerous and more narrow. It's a double-edged tool, according to H. Peter Karoff at the Philanthropic Initiative. "On the one hand, donors want to do something that really helps the organization or issue to get where it wants to go. On the other, conditions are not necessarily driven by what donors think is the case. They may not, for instance, know much about how to run a program for girls in need." The charity, on the other hand, likely knows a great deal.

Frequently, nonprofits are forced to gear up an entirely new program simply to satisfy a donor's requirements. Or they must divert scant resources and expertise from already established, successful programs in order to meet a donor's conditional demands. The organization may need to train staff in different skills or to hire new experts to fulfill your requests, which isn't necessarily the best use of their funds or yours. So the disadvantages of restrictions are that they often work against a donor's real intention, which, of course, is to deepen the impact of funding and make sure that their money is well spent.

"For the sake of results, certainly sometimes, it's good to restrict a donation to a specific program," says Gary, who is also the author of *Inspired Legacies*, a guide to creating a giving plan. "But even then, I recommend giving at least 20 percent to 25 percent of that contribution to assure that core programs and the administration of the organization are covered and that they have a plan to raise more money to cover your grant or gift."

Instead of putting restrictions on a gift willy-nilly, schedule a frank, up-front conversation. "Have a discussion with the organization's executive director to talk about your ideas and their needs," suggests Gary. "Usually an agreement can be reached. If you have concerns about the leadership or its decisions, discuss it with the board chair. I suggest that more of us trust our organizations and leaders and not tie up the money. Too few foundations give to support the capacity and the strategic goals and objectives already mapped out by nonprofits. These leaders have spent years and many hours refining their craft and their goals."

Organizational staff and directors surely need to be held accountable, and you have every right to dictate where your money goes. Still, it's well worth your time and money to learn what the charity is working on and how it's going about it before setting conditions. You may change your mind.

Q&A: Advice from the Multimillionaire Tech Entrepreneur Who Went Social

In 1996, Jeffrey Skoll became eBay's first president and first full-time employee. Two years later, just before eBay went public, he created the eBay Foundation, with some pre-IPO (initial public offering) shares, a lucrative innovation that soon became a model around the country. In 1999, at age thirty-four, Skoll launched his own foundation to focus full-time on social entrepreneurship—that is, finding new and creative solutions for intractable social challenges. These days he also backs movies with a message. He has helped produce George Clooney's *Good Night, and Good Luck* (2005); *North Country*, starring Charlize Theron (2005); Al Gore's *An Inconvenient Truth* (2006); *The Kite Runner* (2007); and Mike Nichols's *Charlie Wilson's War*, starring Tom Hanks (2007). Here's how Skoll decides who and what to support.

Q: *What motivated you to become a full-time philanthropist?*

Skoll: I had spent a lot of time as a kid reading books by Aldous Huxley, James Michener, and Ayn Rand, among others. So by the age of 13 or 14, I had formed a real worldview. It seemed to me then that there were all these trends in the world—overpopulation, terrible new weapons, scary diseases. It also seemed to me that most of the problems were caused by the gap between rich and poor—whether nations, companies or people. I knew that if I ever had significant financial resources, I would want to use them to try to address some of the issues that kept the rich and poor so far apart.

Q: *And what made you back Hollywood films?*

Skoll: I started Participant Productions [a film-producing company] in 2004 because I knew we needed a bigger platform to tell the important stories in a way that I didn't see anyone else in Hollywood doing. Our goal is simple: make compelling movies that highlight important social issues to awaken and inspire audiences to get involved and make a difference. After people see our movies, we want them to say, "Wow! That was powerful. How can I get involved?" The Skoll Foundation, Participant, and

Capricorn, our investment arm, all serve the same vision. We invest in good causes and in change agents who will shape the future. And we try to inspire change through media that, among other audiences, reach the affluent and powerful—the people who can actually do something of value.

Q: *What criteria do you look for in funding an organization?*

Skoll: We're looking for world-class social entrepreneurs with powerful solutions to the world's most urgent problems. There are six areas that we think deserve focused attention, and incidentally, we developed those six issue areas at Participant as well, which serve to integrate the two organizations. These are (1) environmental sustainability; (2) economic and social equity; (3) tolerance and human rights; (4) health; (5) peace and security; and (6) institutional responsibility.

Q: *What due diligence do you require for making a donation? What advice can you offer donors?*

Skoll: Our team goes into the field to assess firsthand the impact of the work. Social entrepreneurs that we support are clear in identifying the goals they want to meet over the term of our grant, which is an initial three years. Regardless of the specific due diligence process a donor or foundation might establish, however, I think it's important to remain open to improving your process over time.

Q: *Do you give by percentage of income, or specific amount, or what the organization requests? Do you restrict gifts?*

Skoll: Our initial Skoll Award is designed to be significant to the organization, but generally will not exceed 20 percent of an operating budget. For a recent round, the award size was $1 million over three years. Our social entrepreneurs appreciate that these awards are for core support and generally not restricted to specific programs or projects. This means they determine the highest and best use of funds.

Q: *What do you require from the organization/cause in return?*

Skoll: We agree up front on their objectives, with both of us signing off on the grant agreement. For example, a social entrepreneur may be well established in India, but seeks to expand to Cambodia. We'll agree on specific milestones for that over the three-year funding period. Hitting the specified milestones triggers award payments. Of course, our team and the social entrepreneurs are in continuous contact, so if things change—and they always do—we can discuss course corrections.

Q: *Is it a good idea to donate anonymously?*

Skoll: I think that's a donor's personal preference and depends on a host of considerations. For me, the more transparent we can be, the better able we are to signal and inspire others to take action. Fundamental to the foundation's mission is that we *celebrate* social entrepreneurs, as well as invest in and connect them. A significant part of our grant making, therefore, involves media initiatives that shine a light on social entrepreneurs and the work they do.

Q: *Do galas and charity balls still play a role?*

Skoll: I actually think those events are opportunities to engage people that might not otherwise be exposed to important work. But the events cannot be about pomp and circumstance. They should be about drawing people into a long-term connection with the work and the organization.

Q: *What lessons have you learned that you can share with donors?*

Skoll: It is important to get started early with small amounts. Figure out what is working and double-down on those things, and keep learning and increasing your bets. One should hope to see results—tangible and rewarding results—in short order! The old style of philanthropy, waiting until you are retired to begin to give away money, is no longer acceptable. The problems today are too urgent and the opportunities to make a strategic contribution now are too great to wait for "retirement" or "a rainy day"!

Chapter 6

HOW DO YOU WANT TO GIVE?

CHOOSING YOUR CHANNEL

L ike nonprofits themselves, the ways you can decide to give money or assets to charity are proliferating. There is no single correct choice. Everything depends on your inclinations and resources. Each alternative for a philanthropic pipeline or method of giving carries its quirks and advantages, tax consequences and legal requirements, specific formats and bits of homework.

The leading options include:

❑ establishing your own private foundation;

❑ creating a personalized fund administered by a community foundation or financial services firm;

❑ giving directly to a public charity or foundation;

❑ participating in a collaborative group or giving circle.

Look for ways to give that most closely match the time, attention, skills, and money you're prepared to invest. Also consider whether your choice offers some growing room, because the rewards of giving have a way of flowing from the experience. Donors typically expand their efforts as they become more engaged.

A Word to the Wise Giver

To pinpoint your preferred method of giving, first become familiar with the pros and cons of the main options described below. After that, tap the experts. Set up an exploratory meeting or two with trusted financial professionals who can help you review circumstances and trade-offs (see Chapter 8 for more on the different kinds of advisors). Philanthropy covers a wide sweep of financial and emotional territory, and, once made, some decisions are irrevocable. If you're considering any planned-giving strategy, such as establishing a foundation, get advice about the financial consequences.

To get you started, here is a roundup of the most popular giving options.

Pros and Cons of Family Foundations

In spirit, family foundations haven't changed much since Andrew Carnegie funded America's first free libraries in the

1890s. Now as then, families of means harness private wealth to promote the public good. As ever, family foundations remain a stately solution to the nasty bite of taxes.

But in all other ways, family foundations are rocking. A record number of first-generation donors are forming private foundations. As of 2006, the latest data available, there were nearly 36,000 family or private foundations, with nearly three out of ten of those (27 percent) established since 2000, according to the Foundation Center, based in New York. (Altogether, in 2007, the more than 72,000 grant-making foundations in the country donated a record $43 billion.) In addition, more family foundations are being formed by people in their forties and fifties who want to be involved in giving during their lifetimes, rather than establishing foundations later as a legacy for heirs. Giving by family foundations reached $16 billion in 2006, up 13 percent from the previous year, and is likely to continue to rise even as the economy sours.

The Foundation Center's Steven Lawrence, senior director of research, notes that since 1975, when the center began collecting data on all grant-making private and community foundations, the country has experienced several downturns. "During each of these recessionary periods—1980, 1981-2, 1990-1, and 2001—U.S. foundation giving in inflation-adjusted dollars did not decline and, in fact, increased slightly," says Lawrence.

ASSET ALLOCATION

"I try to use my resources to maximize each other and to give people resources to help themselves."
—Teresa Heinz, Heinz Family Philanthropies and the Heinz Endowments

Most Family Foundations Have Less Than $1 Million in Assets

An independent, private family foundation usually holds funds from a single family or source. The majority of them are small. Nearly half (48 percent) award less than $50,000 each year. Six in ten (60 percent) report less than $1 million in assets.

Typically, one or more family members serve as officers or board members, and relatives are involved in governance and management. There are complicated choices to make about structure and asset management. There also are serious IRS rules to obey. For instance, you must give away at least 5 percent of the foundation's assets each year, or, in aggregate, over a five-year period. Because of excesses at some family foundations in years past, recent laws have made private foundations the most restrictive in terms of income-tax charitable deductions and other rules.

The Gates-Buffett Ripple Effect

The Bill & Melinda Gates Foundation, with assets in 2007 of about $39 billion, alone pulled up the nation's 2006 grant-making total by $3 billion or so. That ambitious and unprecedented philanthropic power is having an ongoing impact across the board. "I think there is something of a shift lately, in that people are trying to improve the world," says former Citigroup CEO and philanthropist Sandy Weill, who himself has contributed a staggering half billion dollars to charities. "Bill Gates has made a difference, and when

Warren Buffett decided to give up control and treat his philanthropy in the same intelligent way as he's treated his investments, he set a terrific example." Donors see the benefit of pooling resources for greater effect.

The success and sheer size of the Gates Foundation, with its estimated eventual assets of $60 billion, also confers credibility. Venezuelan philanthropist Patricia Phelps de Cisneros, wife of billionaire media mogul Gustavos Cisneros, works to benefit Latin American communities and has experienced the "Gates effect" firsthand. "When an organization gets a donation from the Gates Foundation, it acts like a seal of approval," she says. For example, in 2006, the small New York nonprofit Aid for AIDS, where Cisneros is a board member, received a Gates grant. Immediately, that opened doors and increased funding for the group. "It had a tremendous impact, like night and day," says Cisneros.

How to Set Up a Family Foundation

Life inside family foundations is as idiosyncratic as families themselves. You'll find friendly advice at the growing crop of foundation membership groups, such as the Council on Foundations, based in Arlington, Virginia, and the Association of Small Foundations, based in Washington, D.C., both of which host frequent educational and networking events for families with foundations. Even so, for the true work of grant making and day-to-day management, you're surprisingly on your own. Here are the major issues to consider before establishing a private foundation.

- **Set clear goals.** There are three key reasons to establish a family foundation, according to Ellen Remmer, president and CEO of the Philanthropic Initiative consultancy. First, "if you care about having a visible presence, the separate institution of a family foundation makes a statement," she says. Second, family foundations can pass on a legacy to the next generation. Third, says Remmer, "a family foundation is more stringent. It gets you on a schedule to make the 5 percent required payout."

- **Consider who is "family."** Boards come in all shapes and sizes. Some exclude cousins and in-laws. Others welcome spouses but prepare scenarios in case of divorce. Such decisions ride on family politics. Executive directors are mostly volunteers, but a fair number of family foundations compensate their directors, whether a family member or a hired professional. Foundations that are less active may find it more efficient to work with an outside consulting service to manage research, paperwork, and compliance issues.

  Many trustee or advisory boards include family friends, attorneys, and, depending on the grant program, specially trained experts. The John Templeton Foundation, founded in 1987 by the late legendary investor Sir John Templeton and now directed by his son, John M. Templeton, Jr., gets advice from dozens of international scientists before giving away $50 million or so a year for scientific research into spiritual matters, including the effectiveness of prayer. "We only grant one out of every five proposals," said Sir John in an interview a few years before his death. "I read through each proposal carefully and make my decision, but I call upon the opinions of a board of distinguished advisors."

◆ **Identify your giving style.** To form a foundation, families often gather the clan, sometimes for a weekend retreat, with an attorney or consultants in tow, to work out operating bylaws and a mission statement. That becomes the guiding light for their choice of grants. Operating bylaws ought to reflect donor intentions, without becoming rigid. You don't want an ongoing grant program that's so restrictive it must fund something that becomes unnecessary or outdated—like research into a vaccine for polio, for example.

But even with clear-cut missions, much foundation work is open to trustee interpretation. When troubadour Harry Chapin died at age thirty-eight in 1981, his wife, Sandy, created a family foundation to honor the singer's work on behalf of the homeless and of world hunger. Nowadays, says son Jason, they spend 10 percent or more of the $1.25 million in assets each year. But they limit annual grants, giving a few hundred dollars to $10,000 for each. "That's a big deal to a lot of organizations," he says. "The idea is to give organizations enough help without totally subsidizing them."

Other foundations target their contributions. "To be effective, a family foundation needs a strategic plan over a three- to five-year period," says Alfred L. Castle, with authority. He is executive director of the Samuel N. and Mary Castle Foundation, which was established in Hawaii in 1894 to support early childhood education and is the nation's oldest family foundation, with assets nearing $49 million.

In other words, giving style is all in the family.

◆ **Heed the mission.** The late cultural critic Dwight MacDonald famously described the Ford Foundation as "a large body of money completely surrounded by people who want some." Trustees say turning down applicants is their toughest work. Clear mission statements can help define appropriate proposals. "I have no problem saying no," says Alan Pesky, of Sun Valley, Idaho, who formed his family foundation in 1986 and later initiated the Boise-based Lee Pesky Learning Center in memory of his son, who died of a brain tumor at age thirty. "I simply say, 'I'm very sorry, but we've made our allocation for the year.'" If applicants persist, Pesky offers a tongue-in-cheek tip: "I say, 'You make a donation to the Lee Pesky Learning Center and I'll do the same for you.'"

Technology Is Changing the Giving (and the Family-Foundation) Landscape

The anytime-anywhere reach of technology, broadband online access, and the economies of scale that such tools can offer is transforming the way philanthropic funds are managed.

For example, conventional wisdom has long dictated that the costs and complexities of launching a family foundation meant it wasn't worth doing unless you had $3 million or more in assets to contribute—or $1 million and a lot of time, interest, and know-how. That's because of start-up and operational expenses, including fees for attorneys, accountants and any hired staff; the cost of ongoing paperwork and responsibilities; and, most important, the effort of administering and overseeing the annual payout. Many donors prefer the flexibility and options conferred by private foundations but figured they couldn't afford the overhead.

Now, however, both for-profit and nonprofit services are beginning to offer sophisticated online ways to manage a family foundation's operating needs. Here are two examples:

♦ At Foundation Source, based in Fairfield, Connecticut, CEO Daniel Schley says his fixed-fee service is cost-effective for establishing a foundation with as little as $250,000 in assets. But he has a big caveat: that's true only if you intend to grow the foundation's assets over time, "to at least $600,000, perhaps when there's a major equity event like the passing of a grandparent." Still, he says, "a lot of families think about setting up a foundation, but they're not completely sure. This way, they can start small and grow slowly to see if the family can stay engaged."

♦ At the Association of Small Foundations (ASF), based in Washington, D.C., you can find support by joining for a

Comparing the Options

The National Philanthropic Trust (NPT), based in Jenkintown, Pennsylvania, is an independent public charity that works to increase philanthropy. The group has developed this chart to help donors compare the three most popular giving options and decide which might best work for them.

	Donor–Advised Funds (DAFs)	Supporting Organizations (SOs)	Private Foundations
Start-up Costs	Little or none (often covered by parent organization). Can be established immediately.	Legal fees and other start-up costs can be substantial. Can take anywhere from three weeks to three months to create.	Legal fees and other start-up costs can be substantial. Typically takes a few months to create.
Tax Deduction Limits for Gifts of Cash*	50% of adjusted gross income.	50% of adjusted gross income.	30% of adjusted gross income.
Tax Deduction Limits for Gifts of Stock or Real Property*	30% of adjusted gross income.	30% of adjusted gross income.	20% of adjusted gross income.
Ongoing Administrative and Management Fees	Varies with parent organization and level of services; typically less than supporting organizations or private foundation.	Varies with choice of supporting organization board and level of services required (typically less than a private foundation, depending on size of SO).	Varies with choice of board, and level of services required (typically 2.5% to 4% per year).
Excise Taxes	None.	None.	Excise tax of 1 percent to 2 percent of net investment income annually.

	Donor–Advised Funds (DAFs)	Supporting Organizations (SOs)	Private Foundations
Valuation of Gifts	Fair market value.	Fair market value.	Fair market value for publicly traded stock; cost basis for all other gifts, including gifts of closely held stock or real property.
Control of Grants and Assets	Donor may recommend grants and investments, but the parent organization makes all final decisions.	Donor may recommend grants and investments, but the parent organization has significant input in all final decisions.	Donor family has complete control of all grant making and investments decisions subject to self-dealing rules.
Required Payout	None.	None, but must demonstrate ongoing support for named public charities or causes.	Must expend 5 percent of net assets' value annually, regardless of how much the assets earn.
Governance and Succession	Donor may name advisors to recommend grants and investments. Donors may also name successors to the account and ensure a continuing legacy.	Opportunities for board selection, and bringing in the next generation. Majority of board must at all times be independent non-family trustees, typicallly appointed by named public charity.	Opportunities for board selection, training and bringing in the next generation are greater. No restrictions regarding who serves on the board.
Perpetuity	DAFs can exist in perpetuity. DAFs revert to the parent organization after the original donors or the succeeding generation passes away if no successors are named.	Supporting organization can exist in perpetuity.	Foundations can exist in perpetuity.

*Any unused deductions may be carried forward up to 5 additional years after the year in which the original contribution is made.

modest annual fee of $495. Among other benefits, you gain access to the association's online tool kit, "Foundation in a Box," which provides sample legal documents, tax and investment advice, networking help, board and governance resources, and more. A small foundation is defined as having a staff of "typically less than three, or no staff at all," says ASF's Karen Engstrom, director of membership outreach. Nonetheless, assets for ASF's 3,100 member foundations range from $250,000 to more than $500 million.

Supporting Organizations: An Alternative to Private Foundations

Donors with sizable assets and a plan for committed giving might consider establishing a supporting organization (SO) instead of a family foundation.

There are several categories of SOs. The one that provides an option for family philanthropy is called Type I. Basically, a Type I SO is a public charity that is subsidiary to another, larger public charity or "supported organization." It's like a charity's junior division. Often, the parent is a local community foundation, but not always. Like a family foundation, you can establish the SO with its own name, mission, and governing structure and decide where and how to invest and grant assets. Its benefits include access to the resources, knowledge, and administration of the parent charity. You also may rate a better tax break with the SO than with a family foundation, and you can avoid a lot of the legal paperwork and administrative expenses, because the SO is managed by the parent organization.

The trade-off is control and flexibility. Your SO board must include a majority of members appointed by the parent organization. Family board members or appointees must be a minority, so the parent controls governance and decision making. But if you choose a parent organization wisely—one with a mission and values closely aligned to your SO—the relationship can work very well. Once again, talk to a knowledgeable financial advisor about the pros and cons before you decide.

Honoring the Forgotten

Giving vehicles serve a wide range of interests and intentions. Besides the broader, more generic options, it's entirely possible to set up a specific nonprofit organization dedicated to your exact interests. Elizabeth Colton has done just that.

"I have to say it took me several years not to be embarrassed by my wealth," says Colton, who inherited money from a family business. She echoes the journey many women of wealth take before taking charge of their money. Today living in San Francisco, Colton has founded the International Museum of Women (imow.org), an online, expanding project that uses technology to offer events, exhibitions, and seminars about women's contributions and history. Colton calls her project a "social change museum that inspires global action." The site routinely attracts millions of visitors from dozens of countries. Recently, the IMOW hosted a rich multimedia exhibition online called *Women, Power and Politics*.

"I was inspired to launch the museum because of my daughter," says Colton. "I wanted her to have a place where she could see the value of women."

Donor-Advised Funds Are Easy, Convenient, and Growing

Establishing your own foundation carries the cachet of serious interest and signals significant charitable dollars. But the option of creating a personalized fund hosted by a third party is attracting ever more donors. That's because such funds are low hassle, high reward, and immediately available.

The fastest-growing type is the donor-advised fund (DAF). These funds are investment accounts that allow you to deposit assets and then donate to charities of your choice. Overall, assets of 103 of the largest DAFs in the United States jumped 25 percent in 2007, topping $23 billion, up from $19 billion in 2006, according to an annual survey of the *Chronicle of Philanthropy*. Charities distributed more than $4 billion in DAF grants, an increase of 24 percent over 2006. The nation's largest DAF, the Fidelity Charitable Gift Fund (a public charity) alone made donor-recommended grants of a whopping $1 billion in 2007, a spike of 24 percent over 2006—the largest since the charity was launched in 1991.

Community foundations may have pioneered the use of DAFs, with the first one reportedly created at the New York Community Trust in 1931. But over the past few decades, dozens of for-profit and nonprofit groups have jumped in to serve the mushrooming market. Most financial services firms, from Bank of America to Charles Schwab, JP Morgan Chase and Citibank or Northern Trust, now offer DAFs (and other charitable funds as well), along with expert advice for would-be clients. In a new twist, firms and hosting non-profits also have begun offering options that allow clients to donate tangible assets, including jewels, silver, cattle, and real estate. Lately, too, community foundations are making up for their lost opportunities in DAF offerings and becoming much more donor-friendly, as you can see in the fund options described below.

DAFs do have some disadvantages to bear in mind. Legally, putting money into a DAF means you've given it to the managing organization. In practice, fund managers invariably rely on donor recommendations, but in reality, you've surrendered legal control. And your decision is irrevocable; you cannot get those assets back. In addition, investment options for assets in DAF accounts tend to be limited.

Community Foundations Are Down the Block and Ramping Up

The world's first community foundation began in Cleveland, Ohio, in 1914, and is still thriving today, with assets of more than $2 billion. The Cleveland Foundation was founded so trustees of the Cleveland Trust Company could focus on grant making for the charitable assets held in the company. Until recently, similar local foundations, which sprang up nationwide, have stayed well under the radar.

But in the past two decades, community foundations—plus the DAFs and other funds they host—have become one of the fastest-growing sectors in philanthropy. From 1990 to 2007, cumulative giving by community foundations jumped a whopping 421 percent, in contrast to 194 percent for independent foundations and 91 percent for corporate funders, according to the Foundation Center. Although their numbers remain small, their influence and their grant making have been mounting. Community foundations make up only 1 percent of all U.S. funders, yet they account for nearly 10 percent of all grant dollars, with the bulk going to education, human services, and arts and culture. From 2006 to 2007, community-foundation giving increased by 14 percent, reaching a robust $4 billion, or nearly double the 2000 amount of $2 billion.

As a tax-exempt public charity, usually established as a trust, a series of trusts, or a not-for-profit corporation, a community foundation serves people living in a specific area and works to improve the quality of life for local citizens. "There is no other mechanism for people to give back to the community, unless they give to a specific institution, like a school or a church," says Janet Topolsky, director of the Rural Philanthropy Development group at the Aspen Institute in Washington, D.C. That's particularly true in geographic regions where the various governments that fund water, schools, roads, and services do not cross city, county, or state borders.

Volunteer boards oversee community foundations, but professionals run them. There are now 717 grant-making

Types of Funds

Community foundations offer a selection of funds that you can either support or establish.

- **Unrestricted funds** Usually the oldest funds at a foundation, these give directors wide discretion over what and where to fund.
- **Field of interest or designated funds** Often established as memorial funds, these support a specific interest, such as medical research, an organization, animals, or an historic landmark—any designated place or cause.
- **Donor-advised funds** The biggest growth category in the field, these are funds over which the donor retains some grant-making privileges and, in some cases, investment decision-making power.
- **Supporting organizations** These are usually independent organizations—including private or family foundations—that partner with a community foundation for help with advice, resources, or financial and administrative tasks.
- **Agency endowment funds** These are funds that a community foundation holds and invests on behalf of nonprofit organizations.
- **Scholarship funds** These provide annual scholarships to local students.
- **Community leadership activities** These are non-grant-making programs and initiatives, such as nonprofit professional development or training, that community foundations create or host to address social issues, educate donors, or encourage local philanthropy.

community foundations across the country, including the behemoth $2 billion New York Community Trust, which was founded back in 1924. But most are small, with assets of $25 million or less, and many are young, formed during the go-go 1990s. Some rural community foundations operate with only a scant $100,000 worth of farm equipment or timber.

Why Set Up a Fund instead of Giving Directly to a Cause?

Community foundations typically offer unusual flexibility and convenience for people with some discretionary dollars who want to make a difference, one they get to measure and control. At most community foundations, you'll find staff who are knowledgeable about the area and can educate you about its needs, interests, and issues. "A private foundation is strictly about grant making, while a community foundation has already identified or established programs you can fund," points out Outi Flynn, director of the Knowledge Center at BoardSource.

Without any setup fee, you can establish one of the half dozen or so types of funds offered by most community foundations. Minimums are usually $5,000, sometimes $10,000. Community foundations do charge administrative fees—usually 1 percent of the money they invest and manage for you—but that's likely less than the expense of running a family foundation. You also gain back-office benefits, tax advantages, and a range of fund and estate-planning options. You can choose to support any number of causes in any annual amount, while skipping past the legal, bookkeeping,

and managerial issues required by private or family foundations. Plus, because of a community foundation's aggregate
funds, the 5 percent payout required by the IRS can come
from any or all of the funds the foundation hosts, not just
yours. So if you're still figuring out your giving plan and want
to delay a grant, you rate a tax benefit for the year you set up
the fund, whether or not you make a grant that year.

Choosing Between Control and Convenience

Deciding between a fund and a foundation usually comes
down to control and convenience, not money. Assuming
you've earmarked as much as $1 million to $2 million for
charity, it makes sense to establish a family foundation if you

◆ want to develop a personal giving program;

◆ expect to be engaged and accountable over many years;

◆ want to involve the next generation or other family members and set up a legacy; and

◆ your giving interest cuts across geographic boundaries.

You Can Also Contribute to a Public Foundation

Unlike private foundations, which receive funding from a
single source (family, individual, or corporation), public

foundations must be funded by several sources to qualify as tax-exempt public entities. Usually, big institutions such as universities, hospitals, museums, churches, scientific research centers, and the like incorporate as a public foundation. Such foundations must receive most of their support from grants, gifts, fees, or other income. Support from investment income is limited to a maximum of one-third of total income. Community foundations are a special form of public foundation.

Why Some Donors Prefer to Remain Anonymous

Publicly attaching your name to a donation is entirely a matter of personal preference, although most people who give like the recognition. It's the unusual major donor who remains in the background. Gifts from high-profile donors can also inspire others to give, lend credibility to the cause, or motivate a matching challenge. Then there's ego. It's gratifying to be seen as a great giver. "Roughly 15 percent to 20 percent of donors don't want their name out there, for various reasons," says H. Peter Karoff at the Philanthropic Initiative. But sometimes there is good reason to remain incognito, and the desire for greater privacy is deepening. Here are some reasons to consider giving anonymously:

♦ You want to avoid a deluge of requests and being solicited by other organizations.

♦ You're modest and don't want publicity.

- Your spiritual or religious beliefs advocate giving privately.

- Your relatives might be resentful or envious. "A family member may want to support causes that might embarrass or anger other members of the family," says Diana Aviv, chief executive at Independent Sector.

- "It's useful to give money anonymously when you're asking for a matching donation or a gift in kind," says philanthropist Sandy Weill. "That gives the other donor 100 percent of the credit, while you stay in the background."

If you choose to remain anonymous, send a letter to the leadership of the organization, advises donor-activist Tracy Gary. "Let them know the specifics of your instructions, and ask them to keep the letter in your donor file for future staff to understand. There are degrees of anonymity, so be sure to make your instructions and limitations clear." If you think a conversation with the organization's development officer or executive director will do the trick, think again. Staff turn over frequently.

The Rise of the Fourth Sector and Corporate Philanthropy

Lately, social responsibility is gaining marketplace currency. From global conglomerates to the shop down the block, enterprises are increasing charitable giving, while making sure to market their virtue in doing so. Such efforts are creating a so-called fourth sector.

Giving from large, multinational corporations rose by almost 6 percent from 2006 to 2007, from a median of $25 million to $26 million, according to the annual survey by the Committee Encouraging Corporate Philanthropy, a group cofounded by the late actor and activist Paul Newman.

Motives cover a lot of territory. Some corporate moves are purely philanthropic. For instance, early in 2008, Goldman Sachs earmarked an extraordinary $100 million to teach entrepreneurship and business to women in developing countries. More often, the fourth sector is an umbrella for several blended approaches that go by varying labels, from "social entrepreneurship" and "hybrid" or "for-profit philanthropy" to the infelicitous "philanthrocapitalism" and "philanthropreneurship." Whatever the moniker, the hallmark of such giving is a combination of altruism, pragmatism, and marketing.

Q&A: Finding the Fuel That Lights a Personal Fire

Social entrepreneur Jody R. Weiss, for example, is banking on the simple act of buying lipstick to help women around the globe.

In the early 1990s, after years as a successful sports agent, Weiss found herself at a crossroads. She vividly remembers the moment: She was in Budapest in 1989, watching as

Javier Sotomayor, a Cuban athlete she represented, broke the world's high-jump record. "It was the first time in twenty years that Cubans had competed, because of the ban," she says. "The stadium of 80,000 people went insane—and I didn't care."

At the time, Weiss represented forty-five elite athletes. In a half dozen years, she had built an international reputation as a powerful agent in track and field. "I had a million-dollar budget from Mazda to sign any athlete I wanted." But all she can remember thinking was, "If I have to spend the next few years watching people running around in circles faster and faster, I'll shoot myself." Looking back, she realizes, "It wasn't where my fire was." Having grown up in a socially activist family in the New York area, Weiss figured it was time to reengage. Still, it took some time before she figured out what to do next.

Then, in 2001, she launched PeaceKeeper Cause-Metics—a line of lipsticks, nail polishes, and lip glosses, all free of any potentially harmful chemicals—which donates a percentage of its gross revenues and all after-tax profits to support human rights and women's advocacy issues. Today, the PeaceKeeper Cause-Metics line can be found in Whole Foods Markets, Earth Fare supermarkets, spas, and upscale salons and boutiques around the country. The company has also gone international, with retail distribution deals in Canada and the United Kingdom. As Weiss puts it, "I've found my mojo."

Here's a close-up look at what it takes to launch and run a socially conscious company.

Q: *How do you define Cause-Metics?*

Weiss: Early on, I was talking to the trade team and the term just popped up. I liked it and kept using it. Now we've trademarked Cause-Metics to distinguish PeaceKeeper from other cosmetics companies. A lot of cosmetic marketers give to charity, but it's usually profit from one product or for a limited time. MAC cosmetics gives profits from several lipsticks to AIDS research, and they've now raised more than $115 million. I admire that work. But the difference for PeaceKeeper is that we give away all profits all year long from all of our products— not just for some.

Q: *What led you to launch PeaceKeeper?*

Weiss: There were really two things. The first was that realization in Budapest. I was bored with being a sports agent. But it took a few years before I left, and then I stayed in the field of sports marketing as a consultant.

In 1996, I was in Atlanta, trying to make some money around the Olympics, and I happened to see a photo in a *Time* magazine article. It was a picture of a little girl kneeling on a kitchen table. She was wearing patent leather shoes and there were ruffles around her socks. She had on a beautiful ruffled skirt and her head was back, with the skirt pulled up to her mouth. And she was just wailing. The adults around her were all laughing and applauding. The image was so startling that I read the caption. And found out that it was about female genital mutilation. Of course, I knew that such a thing happened. But somehow, at the time, I didn't know it happened to little girls wearing patent leather shoes in nice kitchens.

So while I kept working, I began writing a screenplay called *The Choice*, about a young woman fighting against the practice.

After the Olympics, I spent some money to produce the film and also looked for a better platform to fight such abuses. The only model that kept wowing me was Paul Newman and Newman's Own foods. If he could give away $100 million to charity on popcorn—which is what it was then; now it's over $200 million—then think of women's enormous buying power.

If every woman in the U.S. were to buy just one PeaceKeeper product a year, we would be able to give millions of dollars to women who can't afford to buy even one lipstick.

Q: *Was it tough to get started?*

Weiss: The hardest part was becoming a chemistry expert. I spent 1998 and '99 researching clean cosmetics, going to organic shows in Germany and so forth. I had to know enough to tell experts what I would and wouldn't stand for in my products. American chemists are 15 years behind the European Union, but even with European chemists, I had to take the lead and tell experts how to push the envelope. They kept telling me it wasn't possible—that I couldn't make such formulations without using certain chemicals. But we did.

Q: *Was it hard to get into upscale retailers? What kind of reception did you get?*

Weiss: The first line was ready in October 2001, a month after 9/11. We had 12 lipsticks and 10 nail polishes, no lip gloss at all yet. I took the finished product to a buyer at Henri Bendel [New York's prestigious boutique department store], and they bought it on the spot.

We were on fire after that. The next month I went to Los Angeles and met with Fred Segal on Melrose ["Where the stars shop"]. He bought it on the spot. A month after that to Nordstrom—they bought on the spot, too.

It is hard to get into such places, but I had years of training as a sports agent in how to ask aggressively. And it was right after 9/11, when the media and TV images were full of issues about the Taliban and how they abused women. We were advocating for women with our products. It was a no-brainer for the retailers.

Q: *How do you allocate which money goes into the business and which goes to causes?*

Weiss: First, we give away pre-profit money of half of 1 percent of all gross revenues. Then we give all profits after taxes. Profit is defined as the money after the cost of projects, PR, marketing, the cost of goods and salaries— everything it takes to run the company, pay taxes, pay any debt to lenders and banks, and financing costs. We also retain transparent working capital to grow the company. Money that would typically be distributed to shareholders then goes to charity.

But we're not yet fully funded or profitable. So it's very frustrating. We need more funding. Women need to be doing for each other. We've given away about $20,000 a year, and we hope to be profitable in a few more years.

We couldn't be broader in our support. We give to eight women's health issues and eight human rights issues that work to stop trafficking and human slavery.

Q: *What would you advise anyone thinking of starting a similar kind of company—if only a kitchen-table version?*

Weiss: I would take his or her temperature. It's hard, baby, the hardest thing I've ever done. I'd have to say, look at the fact that you need all the necessary skills to run a business. This is not a nonprofit. It's a business. It will take over your life.

Google's For-Profit Nonprofit Venture

One of the most high-profile recent examples of corporate philanthropy is Google's DotOrg initiative—officially, Google.org. The project grew out of the well-known pledge made by founders Larry Page and Sergey Brin when the company went public in 2004. At the time, the well-heeled pair promised to reserve 1 percent of their total profits to "make the world a better place." However, it wasn't until January 2008 that the effort launched. Google.org will rely on hybrid philanthropy to fund both nonprofit and for-profit companies to "address the global challenges of our age: climate change, poverty and emerging disease." The company initiative does include a traditional nonprofit, the Google Foundation, which will presumably make conventional grants. But DotOrg is set up to invest capital in small- and medium-size for-profit businesses in the developing world that might help with the problems Google has targeted. DotOrg will spend $175 million in an initial round of grants and investments through 2011—still multimillions short of 1 percent of Google's massive profits.

Doing Well and Doing Good at the Same Time

Another inspirational corporate-giving model has been going strong for a decade, at the Timberland Company, the $1.5 billion international footwear and apparel maker based in Stratham, New Hampshire. "I am responsible for maximizing profit and for a superior return on investment to the shareholder," says Jeffrey Swartz, Timberland's chief executive. "But commerce and justice are not sequential. They're linked."

Swartz, now in his mid-forties, took the helm of Timberland in 1998, having worked in all areas of the company, which was founded by his grandfather Nathan more than a half century ago. Swartz's ideas about for-profit companies "doing well and doing good"—that is, being committed to profits as well as social justice—began serendipitously ten years earlier, when he casually agreed to volunteer for a few hours at a local youth organization. Recounting the experience later, he says, "I found myself, not a mile from our headquarters, face-to-face with the stories you read about in the newspaper. I spent four hours with young recovering drug addicts in a group home. I painted some walls—and felt the world shaking under my feet." Swartz emerged from the experience with a newfound mission.

There was no good reason, Swartz figured, for community service and profitable business to be mutually exclusive. More to the point, he decided that Timberland would emphasize both values every working day.

Consistently voted one of the hundred best places to work by *Fortune* magazine, the company has institutionalized ways for employees to volunteer, mostly through its core Path of Service program. Each employee is allowed forty hours of annual paid leave for community service. Throughout the year, employees organize company-service days, such as a trip to New York to help restore a run-down playground in Queens.

In 1997, the company launched Serv-A-Palooza. At this international yearly event, thousands of employees, vendors, community partners, and young people come together for a day of community service, in company locations around the world. "For one full day, the sun never sets on Timberland service," says Swartz. And in 2002, Timberland launched Service Sabbatical, which encourages employees to put their professional skills to work for community needs for three to six months. One employee worked in a Peruvian orphanage for several weeks, while another used the time to help found a local charter school. Each year, up to thirty employees are also granted leave to spend a few weeks helping disaster relief. Worldwide, the company says its employees have donated more than 300,000 service hours, in some twenty-five countries, in the past decade or so.

As an early advocate for socially responsible corporations, Swartz now finds himself in high-profile company. In 2003, for instance, he and eighteen other CEOs, from corporations like Citigroup, the Home Depot, and Wachovia, were appointed to a presidential task force to investigate ways to expand businesses' community service. "We have clear language for financial performance," says Swartz. "But there's no equivalent language to benchmark the competitive advantage of advocating for human rights, or the environment, or children's rights. There's a huge requirement to galvanize consumers to act more like citizens. Timberland wouldn't be so anomalous if there were more pressure from the marketplace."

Buying for the Social Good—and Selling Product

Other fourth-sector efforts are a dizzying blend of goals and interests, such as the related and rising trend in cause marketing and sponsorships. Such campaigns link a company's products or services to not-for-profit causes or groups in order to leverage the virtues of giving to a cause, burnish the for-profit's brand, sell its products, and do some good, all at the same time. These growing partnerships can "exponentially increase sales, resulting in millions of dollars in potential revenue for brands," according to the 2008 Cone/Duke University Behavioral Cause Study.

American Express first came up with the idea back in 1983. For several months, each time a cardholder charged an item, the company donated a penny toward restoring the Statue of Liberty. The result was a few million dollars to refurbish the Lady—plus glowing press, consumer goodwill, and increased sales for AmEx. Since then, strategies and revenue for cause marketing have skyrocketed. In 2008, U.S. spending on cause marketing is expected to hit $1.5 billion, up more than 4 percent from 2007, according to the *IEG Sponsorship Report.*

The huge international project named (RED), for instance, cofounded in 2006 by U2 lead singer Bono and Kennedy-clan scion Bobby Shriver, who runs a nonprofit that does work in Africa, was created to fight AIDS. Sponsoring companies—including Apple, Emporio Armani, Hallmark, Motorola, and the Gap—all are banking on their (RED) association to impress consumers and boost sales, as well as to support a cause. In 2007, *Advertising Age* magazine reported that the marketing costs for (RED) ran $100 million. And the total raised to fight AIDS? A scant $18 million. Of course, that was $18 million no one had previously.

On the flip side, larger charities are picking up the tools of marketplace branding and using these to generate profile and revenue, too. The biggest nonprofits are spending nearly $8 billion per year on branding, marketing, and public relations, according to a 2006 study by fund-raising consultancy Changing Our World. (The survey examined the Form 990s of seventy-one nonprofits with revenues of $10 million or more and calculated the amount based on itemized deductions.) What we're looking at, posited Changing Our World analysts, is the rise of the charity "product," or nonprofit brands that attract major dollars and "scale up quickly," like the Lance Armstrong Foundation's LiveStrong campaign or the Susan G. Komen Breast Cancer Foundation.

None of this is necessarily a bad thing, especially in an age when it's so tough for any one cause or nonprofit to stand out from the crowd. However, it does argue a need for taking it slow and donor or consumer caution. Just because you've heard buzz about a nonprofit "brand" doesn't mean that organization is doing a good job. Even for larger, more visible charities, due diligence is in order.

How You Can Leverage Corporate-Giving Efforts

Much of the time, fourth-sector activities are about putting values into action. They have good intentions. Given the difficulties nonprofits continue to have in demonstrating their success and impact, hybrid philanthropy is likely to build. You can take advantage of the fourth-sector trend in several ways.

As an employee of a large company, you can bring causes or nonprofit groups to your employer's attention to forge new alliances or set up volunteer programs and options. Check with the HR department or marketing division to find out what's currently in the works. As an entrepreneur or small-business owner, you can institute ongoing charitable projects and engage your staff or associates, whether by donating time, skills, money, or the products and services you sell. You can also build partnerships with several smaller firms or nonprofit organizations to gain impact and build resources. For instance, gather together some peers and launch a campaign for the cause of your choice by using the muscle of your industry or professional association.

Giving Together Encourages Hands-on Philanthropy

Once, giving back was as natural as knowing your neighbors. Everyone pitched in to raise a barn, fund the schoolhouse, or bridge the hard times. Nowadays, that neighborly impulse is resurfacing as an expanding nationwide movement loosely known as "collective giving."

The unifying theme is the idea that pooling resources can lead to bigger grants and greater impact. Collective-giving groups frequently leverage so-called social venture capital, such as members' entrepreneurial skills or professional knowledge, networking contacts and abilities, time and technology. They might, for example, look to local businesses for meeting spaces and supplies. Usually, the collective groups focus on need in their local communities, but not always. The mission of the Clarence Foundation, based in Oakland, California, is to promote philanthropy by helping to start small, egalitarian giving groups around the world, particularly in Africa.

One Person + One Vote + Many Women = Impact

Colleen Willoughby, a pioneer of the collective-giving movement, founded the Washington Women's Foundation (WWF) in Seattle in 1995, with 116 members. The foundation has now grown to 475 members, including Melinda Gates, and has awarded grants of nearly $8 million. Willoughby has gone on to help launch half a dozen similar foundations around the country. Her template for WWF was also the model for Paul Brainerd's well-known Social Venture Partners (SVP) network, an organization that began in Seattle in 1997 and now has dozens of branches around the world. SVP helps nonprofits by providing the collective assets and professional and technological expertise of its members.

For Willoughby, the lightbulb went on after four decades of work as a volunteer leader, including with the United Way. In the mid-nineties, she began thinking about the growing wealth of women. "This is the first generation where a significant number of women are wealth generators as well as inheritors, either by virtue of family or spouse," she says.

"Yet women were not giving up to their capacity or potential. And the needs of the community are not diminishing—they are growing."

"To correct this disconnect," she conceived of launching an incorporated nonprofit that would be dedicated to expanding women's role in philanthropy via pooled contributions and shared decisions. "You can't respond if you don't know," says Willoughby. "Education is critical." At the time, the woman-only focus was innovative enough. The one-person, one-vote collective was altogether radical.

Today, each WWF member makes an annual $2,300 contribution, with a five-year commitment. The foundation grants $1,000 of each contribution to programs voted on by the members every year. Another $1,000 goes to any three 501(c)(3), or tax-exempt organizations, of the member's choosing. The remaining $300 is earmarked for educational programs for members. "The foundation brings women together to accomplish greater goals than any single individual could do alone," says Willoughby, now in her early seventies. "My $2,000 has a $1 million impact."

While membership is limited to women, WWF donations are gender-neutral, funding arts and culture, education, health, and social services. Says Willoughby, "When I launched, there were women's funds supporting women's social justice causes and issues, but no organized ways for women to learn about philanthropy or to financially support community building together. WWF broadened the lens on what has been thought of as 'women's issues.' All issues are women's issues."

Some members participate in foundation events and serve on committees; others simply ante up and vote each year on grant proposals. "The model is easy to set up and fits today's complicated lifestyle by being flexible, with no requirements," says Willoughby. "It offers choices to become more knowledgeable and lets people begin personal community engagement when time is at a premium."

An On-Ramp for Becoming Engaged

Although more structured and thought-out, WWF basically operates like a giving circle. This form of collective giving began in the early nineties and has been a fast-growing grassroots phenomenon. Most circles have launched since 2000.

Democratic and peer-to-peer, like the nationwide book clubs and investment clubs that have flourished in recent years, circles bring Americans full cycle. They resurrect the hands-on help of pioneer homesteading and the legacies of traditional mutual-aid societies—which combine everyone's resources to serve the community—found in Asia and Africa. Circles work by consensus. Members share decisions about the causes they fund. Their egalitarian nature makes them particularly attractive to new donors, especially women and people of color.

"Giving circles work because there are no hurdles to being involved," says philanthropy consultant Darryl Lester, who founded the Next Generation of African American Philanthropists (NGAAP), a twenty-nine-member circle in Raleigh, North Carolina, in 2003. "We want to create an on-ramp for the time, talent and treasure it takes to be critically engaged in the community. It's about empowerment."

Why Darryl Lester Quit His Job to Focus on Giving Circles

After years as a student-affairs administrator at universities and a program director for community foundations, Darryl Lester got the message. "Whenever people talked about who was philanthropic, it was always folks in a certain part of town," he says. "African Americans were never on the supply side of philanthropy. They were only on the demand side. I struggled with that."

In 2001, Lester walked away from big institutions to work on changing that image. "I deal with the mindset that philanthropy is what someone else does," he says. "But the motivations for giving are the same for everyone. People give to be recognized and connected to certain things. When you break philanthropy into its three tenets—time, talent, and treasure—that resonates with people. You have to be willing to ask."

Nowadays, in his mid-forties and based in Raleigh, Lester travels the South, putting his mouth and livelihood where his heart and mind ended up. "I was raised in a small rural community that understood that sacrifices come with the things you inherit. I realized that organizing and talking to friends about making a change in the world is something I actually believe in."

Lester's key tool in developing philanthropy in black communities has been organizing giving circles. His initial circle, NGAAP, mostly consists of married couples like Lester and his wife, Dionne, an electrical engineer. The required annual donation is $250, though many give more. "It was a little tough at first," says Lester. "But by now people have seen the difference they've created. In the philanthropic world, a small grant doesn't have major impact. But when grassroots organizations receive grants of $500 to $1,000 to support staff development or to earn matching gifts from a foundation, the ripple effects are more than the dollars."

NGAAP grants average about $11,000 a year. Recent awards went to a residence for African American women with AIDS, a group that helps teens suspended from school, and a program offering computer classes for single moms and their kids. Another grant went to pay travel expenses for a group of formerly homeless people who had launched an organization to help those still homeless in the community. The group's founders had been invited to testify before Congress about their successful efforts but could not afford the trip without the grant.

Since 2003, Lester has helped to launch eleven circles, including the all-women Zawadi group in New Orleans, which suffered the Katrina diaspora and recently regrouped; a Virginia group with members from several generations; the

Heritage Quilters, a rural-craftswomen group in Warrenton, North Carolina; and a coed group of young professionals in Charlotte.

"Giving circles change the face of what a donor looks like in the community," says Lester. "I want philanthropists to look like Darryl Lester."

Circles Are Casual, Effective, and Social

At last count, in 2007, the country's 400 or so giving circles had raised an amazing $100 million to meet the needs of their communities—with more circles forming every year, according to New Ventures in Philanthropy, in Washington, D.C., the research arm of the Forum of Regional Associations of Grantmakers. That's up from about 200 in 2004.

Circles have sprung up in places like Moscow, Idaho; Angleton, Texas; as well as in Chicago, Los Angeles, and New York. Some consist of five or so friends who get together in someone's dining room for a potluck dinner a few times a year. Others are hosted by community foundations or have evolved into stand-alone 400-member organizations with legal nonprofit status, structured committees, and bylaws, like the WWF. Often, circles ask donors to commit to giving for a few years so that the group can gain consistent grantmaking experience. But contributions range widely, from as little as $100 to as much as $100,000 a year. Some circles require an annual minimum contribution, while others set up optional tiered recommendations. Still others leave the amount entirely up to each member.

In fact, one of the major attractions of giving circles, and a reason they're growing so fast, is their flexibility. If donors decide the rules aren't working, they simply change course.

Circle participants usually want to do more than simply write checks. Members typically visit organizations or community programs to learn about the issues in their communities, often inviting local educators or foundation directors to talk to them. Members review proposals for funding, determine how much money to give, and work together to make the grants. Many giving circles follow their grantees over time to review how the money is being used.

What giving circles share is a personal and highly participatory experience for people looking to make a difference. Says Lester, "Folks who come to a circle may not have a great deal of access or surplus, but everyone has substance. Circles let people use that substance to learn the whole range of how giving takes place in the community." Most people join circles for social as well as philanthropic reasons. That's a very different experience than writing a check to behemoth groups like, say, the Red Cross.

"Foundations tend to take themselves and their tasks very seriously—and rightly so," says Hank Doll, who, along with his wife, Mary, founded the Giving Back Gang in Shaker Heights, Ohio, in 2003. "But this is a way to study the community, have fun with people you know, and make a real difference." Doll's circle has fifteen members. "We started at

Seven Steps to Starting a Giving Circle

Like any group effort, giving circles demand time and resources. Start slowly by meeting with interested friends or colleagues and thinking through these options.

1. Decide on the giving circle's mission and focus. Do you want to decide on a mission up front or recruit members and then figure it out as a group?

2. Set priorities for grant making. Do you want to stick to a single issue or location?

3. Define the circle's format and structure. Circles often average thirty to forty members, but they vary. At the kickoff meeting, you'll want to consider how often the group will meet, whether attendance should be required, and how decisions will be made. You may also think about an alliance with a host institution, such as a foundation or sponsor.

4. Determine the level of commitment. How much money, time, and expertise are expected?

5. Choose a home for the money. Will you open a separate bank account or ask an institutional host to manage it? If grants come directly from each member's contribution, make sure individual checks are made payable to a nonprofit grantee rather than another circle member. That way, everyone rates a charitable tax deduction.

6. Delegate the tasks. Who will be responsible for what?

7. Don't forget expenses. Some funds will be needed to cover materials, food, postage, financial arrangements, and so on.

$500 contributions, but interest was so great we increased it to $1,000 a year."

The Giving Back Gang focuses on public education, and its first grant went to a Cleveland school puppetry program designed to help kids and parents handle emotional issues. "All the handheld puppets are made by parents and kids. So four of us showed up to help make them," says Doll, who is in his early seventies. "It was a wonderful evening." All in all, he says, "We're having a blast."

Chapter 7

WHAT ABOUT FINANCES?

MANAGING TAXES AND TRUSTS

D espite all the highfalutin images of philanthropy—the white-glove society donors, the
glitzy galas, the newly minted Silicon Valley
billionaires—it remains supremely true that trying to effect
change is never about how much money you have or the
amount you donate. What then?

It's about a decision. You decide to step over the threshold
to join the ranks of people who look for solutions instead of
just cataloguing problems. You decide it's time. You wield
the power of one.

Yes, It's Simpler to Write a Check, but Is It Smarter?

But if philanthropy does not require gobs of cash, it is
nonetheless both wiser and more effective to craft a

"Increasingly in the past five years people are asking, 'How can I make a difference that speaks to the legacy I want to leave in the world?' Women and men are giving at a level of significance and meaningfulness to them. They're giving as part of our legacy in the world, and as a daily footprint, rather than after we die, in order to make a current and physical impact. It's altering the landscape of philanthropy."
—ANA OLIVEIRA, PRESIDENT, NEW YORK WOMEN'S FOUNDATION

customized financial plan before you begin. A plan can help maximize the impact of your gift, both right away and in years to come. It also pays to define exactly what income and categories of assets you possess, how much those assets are worth (today and down the line, if and when they appreciate), and whether they are being appropriately managed and leveraged—for your family and your future, as well as for philanthropy.

"This isn't just a discussion about what's on paper," explains Candace Bahr, a wealth manager who runs the Bahr Investment Group, in the San Diego area. "You need to talk about inflation and its effects, how to manage all the separate money and investment accounts and so on. The problem of managing money by simply following the markets is that people get caught up in the emotion of it. There's so much noise constantly coming at you, it's difficult to differentiate the noise from the real information."

Then, too, while charity primarily flows from a desire to further a cause, you can realize significant tax savings and advantages from your gifts. Why not put tax strategies into place that will yield the most benefit? A financial pro or two can help, whether an accountant, a tax attorney, or an estate or financial planner, as can a planned-giving officer or a philanthropy consultant (see Chapter 8 for more on choosing advisors). Getting a solid handle on your personal finances usually leads to greater ease in giving, especially as you get older and likely have more assets to grow and protect. "Lately, and especially since 9/11," says Stephanie Ackler at Ackler Wealth Management in New York, "as people's pot and asset base get bigger, I find them asking, 'What percentage of assets can I afford to give, and what structure makes sense?'" When those questions have specific answers, all sorts of financial decisions get easier.

The New Rules for Charitable Tax Savings

The most sweeping changes to charitable giving in recent memory kicked in when Congress passed the Pension Protection Act of 2006, a law intended to encourage more giving, ease some rules, and prevent abuse by making non-profits more accountable. Before making any contribution, ask your accountant, tax attorney, or money manager about how those changes might affect you.

Tax deductions reduce the cost of your donation, of course. Contributions to qualified organizations may rate a deduction against income taxes, if itemized, only for the year in which you make them. Assuming a 33 percent tax bracket, for example, the cost of a $100 donation to a qualified organization is $67 ($100, less the $33 tax savings). In higher tax brackets, that cost goes down further, making contributions more attractive for bigger taxpayers. Wealthier donors thus receive a greater reward for giving, presumably to encourage them to give more. Limits to deductions are fairly high. Typically, you can deduct cash contributions to charities of up to 50 percent of your adjusted gross income and 30 percent for contributions of stock or property that has appreciated, but it depends, of course, on your circumstances.

List of Deductible Contributions

You can deduct charitable contributions on your income taxes only if you make them to IRS-qualified organizations. An organization's tax-exempt status does not automatically mean that your gift will be tax deductible. Ask before you give.

Deductible as Charitable Contributions	Not Deductible as Charitable Contributions
Money or property you give to:	Money or property you give to:
• Churches, synagogues, temples, mosques, and other religious organizations	• Civic leagues, social and sports clubs, labor unions, and chambers of commerce
• Federal, state, and local government, if your contribution is solely for public purposes (e.g., a gift to reduce the public debt)	• Foreign organizations (except certain Canadian, Israeli, and Mexican charities)
• Nonprofit schools and hospitals	• Groups that are run for personal profit
	• Groups whose purpose is to lobby for law changes
• Public parks and recreation facilities	• Homeowners' associations
• War veterans' groups	• Cost of raffle, bingo, or lottery tickets

Deductible as Charitable Contributions	Not Deductible as Charitable Contributions
• The Salvation Army, Red Cross, CARE, Goodwill Industries, United Way, Boy Scouts, Girl Scouts, Boys and Girls Clubs of America, etc.	• Individuals
	• Political groups or candidates for public office
• Charitable organizations listed as eligible in IRS Publication 78. You can search this database in the "Online Version of Publication 78," on the IRS Web site (www.irs.gov/app/pub-78/).	• Tuition
	• Value of your time or services
• Expenses paid for a student living with you sponsored by a qualified organization	• Value of blood given to a blood bank
• Out-of-pocket expenses when you serve a qualified organization as a volunteer	

Source: IRS.gov

Keep a Paper Trail to Confirm Your Deductions

Since the 2006 law took effect, you can't claim deductions for cash contributions of any kind unless you can back them up. So collect receipts, keep canceled checks or credit card statements, and ask nonprofits for written acknowledgment of any contribution you make, even small amounts. Bank records or receipts must include the name of the charity and the date and amount of every monetary contribution you claim as a tax deduction—including the most casual.

Sizable checks or cash donations are easy to remember

when tax time rolls around. But to get the most from your charitable write-offs, you also need to keep track of smaller contributions and expenses for various good deeds and charitable causes. Keep personal receipts detailing the date and the amount given for even the smallest donations.

Options for Older Donors: Donating Directly from an IRA Account

The Pension Protection Act also mandated a special tax break in 2006 and 2007 for older donors who wanted to contribute directly from qualified tax-deferred accounts. Congress then extended that break in the huge economic rescue package hurriedly passed in October 2008 to alleviate the country's economic crisis.

Taxpayers aged 70½ or older can withdraw as much as $100,000 per year from their individual retirement accounts (IRAs) or Roth IRAs and donate the funds to an eligible charity without incurring any income tax for the distribution. You don't even need to itemize your return to take advantage of this provision (if you do itemize, you can't also deduct the same contribution).

The rule applies only to IRAs, not to other qualified plans, such as 401(k) accounts, SIMPLE IRAs or simplified employee pension (SEP) plans. With some exceptions, this option can be particularly beneficial to high-income donors who choose to make large contributions.

How Deductions Work for Donating Used Goods, Art, and Real Estate

The 2006 law also attached some strings to noncash donations. For instance, you may claim a deduction for used goods, such as clothing, furnishings, electronics, appliances, or linens. But you rate a write-off only for the item's fair market value at the time of the donation. That, of course, is likely to be a whole lot less than what you originally paid, unless it's some kind of collectible. To gain an idea of what your items might be worth, check local thrift shops, second-hand furnishings stores, or on eBay.

To rate a tax deduction for a used item worth $500 or more, the item must be in "good used condition or better." The IRS now requires that a documented qualified appraisal for each such donation be filed with your tax return.

At the higher end of the scale, donations of collectibles and art have changed dramatically under the new law. Previously, these were called "fractional gifts," because donors could contribute 10 percent or so of a work's value each year and then deduct increasing amounts as the art-work appreciated in value. New York's Museum of Modern Art, for instance, has about 650 works in its collection that began as partial gifts. In years past, these were gifts that kept on giving, to, say, a museum, and to the donor's tax benefit. But the Pension Protection Act has put a damper on such gifts. Annual deductions are now limited to relevant percentages of the piece's value at the time of the gift. Similarly, there are tighter rules for contributing fractional interests in tangible personal property, such as antiques.

On the one hand, this adjustment for fractional gifts only seems fair. In the past, many donors willed art to museums or other institutions to gain bigger and better tax write-offs every year, while the public received no benefit until after their death, perhaps decades later. On the other hand, one critic of the change, noted art collector Howard Rachofsky, calls this part of the law unbalanced.

A multimillionaire and retired hedge fund manager, Rachofsky, along with his wife, Cindy, and a few other wealthy couples, transformed the Dallas Museum of Art in 2005 with a collective, irrevocable bequest of 800 artworks, valued at $400 million, including a Monet painting, *Water Lilies—The Clouds*, which alone has been pegged at $25 million.

"There were better ways to draft this legislation," argues Rachofsky, suggesting that the traditional fractional tax deduction might have depended on having an artwork displayed in a public space for a specified period of time rather than simply being left to hang on someone's wall until the donor dies. "As drafted, this law punishes people for trying to do a nice thing," he says.

Tax Incentives for Gifts of Land

The Pension Protection Act's generous tax incentives for land gifts expired with tax year 2007. But Congress extended its provisions through 2009, and they may well be extended again. For now, deductions for land-conservation gifts and historic landmarks, or so-called façade easements, remain bumped up from 30 percent to 50 percent of your adjusted gross income. That can go up to 100 percent for either individuals or corporations if farming or ranching is allowed on the land. In addition, the number of years over which donors can take such deductions has been increased from six to sixteen. But to rate this write-off, you're now required to preserve a building's entire exterior, and you're also prohibited from making any change that may muddle its historic character.

Donations to conservation groups, called land trusts, have resulted in millions of acres of working land and natural areas being conserved for the future, according to Russ Shay, public policy director of the Land Trust Alliance, a national conservation group based in Washington, D.C. Altogether, land trusts in America have saved more than 36 million acres—or an area about the size of New England—from development.

Getting Tax Breaks for Volunteer Work

Don't forget to tally the costs of any volunteer work you do. Generally, you can deduct out-of-pocket expenses for volunteering, including items like supplies, uniforms, highway tolls, stamps, and stationery. You can also deduct the cost of transportation, meals, and lodging if the work for an eligible organization or religious group takes you out of town. You may deduct fares for public transportation, or fourteen cents a mile if you drive your own car while engaged in volunteer work.

You cannot, however, deduct the value of any services you provide. For instance, if you're a graphic designer who creates a brochure for an eligible nonprofit, you can deduct the cost of paper and supplies but not the value of your design work.

Mapping the Territory for Planned Giving

Most people don't think much about "planned giving"—that is, strategic, long-term charity that transfers significant assets and yields valuable tax benefits. Such gifts present lots of options and often call for the advice of financial pros. For instance, many charitable gifts can be set up to throw off income that you live on, while helping you save on taxes. The asset or principal goes to charity only upon your death.

Check with a charity's development officer, a CPA, or an attorney to help you structure a planned-giving vehicle. Gifts can include cash, art, real estate, business interests, appreciated securities, charitable trusts, annuities, and more. You can also determine the timing of the gifts, whether yearly from a charitable trust or as a one-time contribution from a tax-deferred savings account, like an IRA, once you reach the age eligible to tap the money without penalty. You may also choose among a range of bequest and estate options. Possibilities are pretty open-ended. (Also see Chapter 10, about funding a legacy, for more advice on planned giving.)

Still, most people, even donors with charitable track records, typically avoid larger or long-term gifts, likely for the same psychological and financial reasons that keep people from drawing up wills or consulting planners about their estates. In addition, when it comes to serious gifts to charity, many people are concerned—with good reason, mind you—that such contributions are a risky move, because they may need the money in later years to look after themselves or their family.

Often, a decision about planned giving comes down to getting more educated about how much you really have to give. Lawyer Mary Beth Martin, who heads up the Boston office of Changing Our World, a philanthropy consultancy,

A Potential Windfall in Tax Savings

In 2007, Fidelity Investments estimated that the potential additional federal-tax savings for Americans who could donate appreciated securities instead of cash is between $2.2 billion and $4.5 billion annually. "Simply put," says the Fidelity research, "millions of Americans who itemize their charitable deductions could potentially save billions of dollars or give billions more a year to charity if they understood the tax advantages of using appreciated securities they already own—whether they be stocks, bonds or mutual funds—instead of cash to make gifts they already intend to make."

tells the story of a teacher who willed what she thought were her total assets to a charity, about $7,000. But the teacher also included her house, which, it turned out, had appreciated to $300,000. "Donors can have a big impact and don't realize it," says Martin.

Having Your Cake and Your Charity, Too

Currently, the federal estate tax is slated for elimination by 2010, though the federal gift tax will remain. (Basically, these are graduated taxes imposed on the donor of a gift when assets, money, or property are transferred from one person to another, with some exemptions.) All signs point to swift reinstatement of estate taxes by the Congress in 2011, however, so don't hold your breath in the interim. Forecasters expect that the resulting law will remove estate taxes from estates of up to $5 million for individual taxpayers and up to $10 million for couples. That leaves a scant 0.5 percent or so of the country's estates facing a tax burden, according to Susan Raymond at Changing Our World. Presumably, the vast majority of people won't need to worry about it. Still, that's only federal taxes. State and local governments also tax estates, and these assessments vary enormously.

What's key here is, if you make arrangements in advance, money that might other-

CHOICES

"Everyone's a philanthropist, whether an involuntary one when your money goes to Uncle Sam or a voluntary one when you choose to give."
—MARGARET MAY DAMEN, INSTITUTE FOR WOMEN AND WEALTH

wise end up going to taxes and government-determined options could be going to the charities of your choice.

Trusts are especially effective vehicles for realizing tax savings. There are many kinds of trusts that can shelter income for you and the next generation, including revocable or living trusts, irrevocable trusts, supplemental or special needs trusts (which can care for heirs with disabilities), and QTIP (qualified terminal interest property) trusts (which allow surviving spouses to postpone estate taxes). Charitable trusts also come in a variety of flavors, so check with advisors about pros and cons.

Main Benefits of Charitable Remainder Trusts

Despite the many options, when setting up a charitable trust most donors choose the convenience of charitable remainder trusts (CRTs), either a charitable remainder unitrust (CRUT) or a charitable remainder annuity trust (CRAT). The major difference between the two is how the income is paid out.

CRTs, which were mandated by Congress in 1969 to help fund nonprofits, provide for two beneficiaries of the trust's assets: you and the charity you designate. You (and your spouse, if you're married) receive a set percentage of the income generated by those assets during your lifetime. CRTs are irrevocable trusts, meaning you can't change or dissolve one after it's established. But you can change beneficiaries and, if desired, you can keep control of investing the assets.

Ten Facts Every Trust Beneficiary Should Know

" **A**fter years of working with families to establish trusts," says New York–based wealth manager Patricia Angus, "it's become clear that there's a need for better understanding by the persons creating trusts and, more importantly, by beneficiaries, about what a trust is, and how trusts work." As a start to navigating the often complex issues, Angus has developed this list.

The Beneficiary's Rights

To review the trust agreement and related documents

To expect the trustee to be accountable to each beneficiary and remainderperson (someone who has a future interest in the estate) of the trust

To have a trustee who is willing to maintain open communication

To attend regular (or at least annual) meetings with the trustee to discuss trust matters and the beneficiary's personal financial circumstances and goals, and to provide input on the trustee's performance in the light of the trustee's duties and responsibilities

To seek removal of a trustee in appropriate cases

The Beneficiary's Responsibilities

To actively participate in trust affairs

To understand the trust's mission or overriding purpose

To understand his or her rights and responsibilities under the trust agreement and how these relate to the rights and responsibilities of other beneficiaries and remainderpersons

To gain a basic understanding of trust law, including the trustee's roles and responsibilities

To obtain a general understanding of investment fundamentals, the trust's budget, and to know how and in what amount trustees and other professionals are compensated

Typically, CRTs throw off income for trustees, reduce estate and income taxes, shelter income for the next generation, and, when the trustee dies, pass the trust assets to a charitable beneficiary. "CRTs are a great tax-planning tool," says Robert Lew, a San Francisco–based financial planner who specializes in planned giving. "The primary benefits are saving on income taxes while creating income for donors."

Little wonder then that CRTs are now the second fastest-growing charitable-giving vehicle in the country (donor-advised funds rank first). In 2006, the latest IRS figures available, there were about 116,000 CRTs in the United States, accounting for a whopping $105.7 billion in net assets, up from $88 billion in 2005.

Jackie O Chose a Charitable Lead Trust

When Jackie Kennedy Onassis's will became public in the mid-nineties, it turned out that she had relied on a charitable lead trust (CLT) to keep her money active. The CLT not only allowed her to continue to fund her favorite causes after her death but also permitted the transfer of the bulk of her estate to her children without triggering estate taxes. At the time, this type of trust was not well known, primarily because its structure best suits people with major bucks. But thanks to the nation's recent surge in wealth and philanthropy, CLTs are attracting more attention.

A mirror image of the CRT, the CLT reverses the payouts.

In other words, you and your heirs hang on to your assets while a qualified charity receives annual income for the term of the trust, whether for a certain number of years or a lifetime—your choice. That means you can "lend" stock, real estate, or other assets to a charity—which immediately receives gifts of income—without having to give away any property.

Further, when the trust expires, your assets have typically grown in value and can pass to the next generation (or even the one after that) at a tax discount. Of course, any charity that benefits from a CLT is thrilled to be able to bank on consistent annual funding. "Planned gifts, including CLTs, are extraordinarily beneficial to organizations," says Haida McGovern, director of institutional advancement at Women for Women International, a Washington, D.C.–based group that helps women war survivors rebuild their lives. "Once the donor and the charity come to an agreement on what the resources will be used for, CLTs provide an income stream that the organization can count on for a predictable period of time to support its programs."

CLTs also come in two varieties. A charitable lead annuity trust (CLAT) pays the charity a fixed amount of income each year. A charitable lead unitrust (CLUT) pays a percentage of the trust's assets each year. Choosing between these options can be far trickier than it first seems. For instance, if you decide on a fixed amount, you must pay the same amount each year even if your assets shrink dramatically over the term of the trust. Similarly, if you decide on paying a percentage of the assets, your contribution can spiral upward if your investments do well. You need solid advice about which CLT will best work for you.

CLTs are still far from mainstream, but they are growing. In 2006, according to IRS filings, there were about 6,300 CLTs across the country, accounting for net assets of $16 billion, up from 6,100 and $15 billion, respectively, the previous year. And they've jumped 35 percent since 2001. "CLTs are a hot topic as a planning technique," says Grace Allison, tax strategist at Northern Trust. "They are phenomenal devices for leveraging exemptions for gift taxes, estate taxes and the generation skipping tax."

Nevertheless, CLTs require the luxury of being able to afford to lock up your assets for some period of time, forgo the income those assets could generate, *and* pay annual income tax on the trust's earned income (minus the charitable deductions). That's hardly everyone's cup of tea. In theory, any amount of money can establish a CLT, while you tap other income to live on. In practice, CLTs tend to attract people with a healthy threshold of wealth.

So what's driving the increased interest? In the past decade, the nation's pentamillionaires quadrupled, to 1 million, according to an annual survey on wealth from Harrison Group, a market researcher. Some 2.5 percent of the population now has assets of $10 million to $20 million and has been wealthy, on average, for only about fifteen years. This group is getting older, too. More and more well-heeled boomers are eyeing their legacies, using their money to make a difference, and finding ways to shelter hard-earned wealth for future generations.

Given the benefits, CLTs are likely to keep multiplying over the next decade. But, as financial planner Lew points out, "CLTs don't work without charitable intent."

Giving While You Live

Direct funding for women's and girls' concerns still represents less than 7 percent, or about $1 billion, of the largest U.S. foundations' awards to special interest groups, reports the Foundation Center. But a growing group of wealthy activist women have been working to improve that.

In November 2007, Helen LaKelly Hunt, daughter of oil tycoon H. L. Hunt, joined Abby Disney and several other women philanthropists in launching an unprecedented fund raising campaign called Women Moving Millions—invoking both dollars and people. The campaign set a goal of raising $150 million by spring 2009 from individual donors each contributing $1 million or more to fund women's rights, safety, and economic development locally and internationally.

Hunt and her younger sister, Swanee, who directs the Women and Public Policy Program at Harvard University's Kennedy School of Government, cooked up the idea by partnering with the Women's Funding Network (WFN), a member association of 132 women's organizations around the globe. The $150 million target was chosen because WFN organizations have donated a total of $850 million since the group was established in the mid-1970s. As Hunt put it, "giving a billion dollars to fund women's causes had a nice ring."

Luminaries in the women's philanthropy movement, the Hunt sisters have long put their fortunes to work for change. Helen helped found the Dallas Women's Foundation, the Ms. Foundation for Women, the New York Women's Foundation, and the Women's Funding Network. Swanee served as U.S. ambassador to Austria during Bill Clinton's first term and helped negotiate peace in Bosnia. Her foundation, the Hunt Alternatives Fund, based in Cambridge, Massachusetts, focuses on "provoking social change," often beyond American borders. According to Swanee, she's so far given away about $125 million—$60 million in direct grants and $65 million awaiting disbursement through her foundation. "About $40 million of it has gone to fund women's activities," she says.

But Swanee wasn't always ready to donate so much. In 2005, she was anticipating taking a diplomatic job in Liberia (which ultimately didn't materialize). "It's easy to die in a war zone," she says. So she made sure her affairs were in order. "I went over the will and thought, 'Well, Helen is the godmother of women's philanthropy, in terms of living people, so I should leave her $5 million for her work.' I got all teary talking to the lawyers and thought how beautiful it would be when Helen hears about this and I'm dead."

Then it dawned on Swanee that she might outlive her sister—or that by the time Helen inherited, she might be too old to do the work. "That was the turning point," says Swanee. "I realized I could do this right now." Each year,

Swanee puts half of her income from portfolio earnings into her foundation. "Change," says Swanee, "is not only what's in your pocket. It's also what's in your heart." Ultimately, the Hunts kicked off the Women Moving Millions campaign with a combined grant of $10 million of their own—$6 million from Swanee and $4 million from Helen.

By fall 2008, the effort had reeled in $110 million from 56 donors—including two men—around the world, and the $150 million goal was within reach. Donors, who represent a range of wealth and female star power, include former Cisco Systems senior marketing officer Catherine Muther; New York philanthropist Liz Sackler, whose father, Arthur Sackler, was a legendary philanthropist himself; and actress Jane Fonda.

Chapter 8

WHO CAN YOU ASK FOR HELP?

ADVISORS COME IN ALL SIZES

Philanthropy is now big business—a $306 billion industry, in fact. "A by-product of all the money in the water is that there are a lot of people who want to get in on the relationship between the donor and the charity," says Trent Stamp, former president of watchdog group Charity Navigator. Enter the philanthropy or donor consultant.

Such consultants first surfaced in the seventies, but the field really took off in the booming nineties. And today, as so many more Americans tap specialized financial experts to help manage their personal finances, philanthropy consultants are joining the family money team, bringing different perspectives and expertise to the mix.

That's because, although financial planners may be astute advisors about asset allocation, leveraging debt, or insurance needs, they are often seriously out of their depth when it comes to shaping creative structures for planned giving. Likewise, tax attorneys, wealth managers, investment counselors, stock brokers, and estate planners may be terrific within their given arenas, but they are typically unable to provide big-picture judgments on charitable options, tax benefits, payout requirements, legacy plans, or structured gifts to the next generations.

"On a project basis, any time you embark on estate planning, legal issues or a period of concentrated work on a giving plan, a philanthropy consultant can be helpful," says Lee Draper at the Draper Consulting Group in Los Angeles.

Billionaire Sheila Johnson Learned to Target Her Gifts

Sheila C. Johnson, cofounder of Black Entertainment Television (BET), established her private foundation in 1989 with a modest $2 million. After BET was sold to Viacom in 2001 for $3 billion and Johnson divorced her husband and BET cofounder Robert L. Johnson in 2002, she walked away with nearly $1 billion. Her foundation then rapidly expanded. Assets are currently about $23 million and will eventually reach about $100 million. But as the foundation's potential grew, Johnson moved much too quickly. "I had two years of missteps," she acknowledges. As a result, she stepped back and began consulting with philanthropy advisor Diana Chambers, who runs the Chambers Group, in Washington, D.C.

Chambers helped Johnson hone her foundation's mission, which now focuses on the arts, education, and children. Previously, Johnson had been giving somewhat impulsively, and to a wide swath of causes and groups. Johnson also called Bill Gates to hear how the Gateses handled giving efforts. "They made all the mistakes I did. It was very reassuring," she says.

Nowadays, Johnson recommends tapping outside expertise to implement a giving plan that can deliver real change and results. "I have contractual agreements drawn up, and the money is earmarked," she says. In 2005, Johnson hired a full-time foundation director, who, along with Johnson's two grown children and others, recommends possible funding choices and tracks the foundation's grantees and their progress. To date, Johnson, now in her late fifties and remarried, has given away about $20 million, including $7 million to Parsons the New School for Design, in New York, for much-needed building renovations. In 2007, she contributed a high-profile $4 million challenge grant to CARE in support of its "I Am Powerful" global campaign to empower women.

In advising other donors, Johnson says, "Don't get mad at the money because it's not working. Learn how to use it."

How Consultants Weigh In

Typically, philanthropy consultants are hired by donors to guide them through the process of matching their philanthropic intentions with simpatico and worthwhile organizations. As with any personal coach or financial pro, hiring the right one can be incalculably helpful.

"People are tired of buying lots of stuff and they're moving from conspicuous consumption to more conspicuous compassion," says Margaret May Damen at the Institute for Women and Wealth, a legacy-planning service in Palm City, Florida. "Consultants can help motivate donors to give more and to connect with their passion." Good consultants are knowledgeable and up to speed on the current philanthropic horizon. They can serve up options you wouldn't otherwise know about or explore, saving you time, shoe leather, and money. They can help you to determine a comfortable level of engagement.

In addition, consultants can prioritize options for creating a customized giving plan, covering how much and when to give and to which deserving groups. Larger, more sophisticated advisory firms with specialists on staff can go on to measure the effect of large-scale gifts and provide feedback on your impact.

Overall, consultants can steer you onto paths that effectively put your mission and values into action. "Hire one when you're just starting out and when you're at a critical transition, such as when you have money coming in or you're creating a new plan," suggests Ellen Remmer, who is both chief executive at the Philanthropic Initiative consultancy, and a donor and board member of her own family's foundation.

The Remmer Family Foundation provides a good case in

point. Formed in 1992, the small foundation is thriving today, with about $4 million in assets. But the family did undergo some early growing pains, says Susan Remmer Ryzewic, Ellen's sister and the foundation director.

"The first year, we tried to do it on our own, and even though we're smart, we weren't effective," says Ryzewic. "There's always a lot of emotional baggage and complicated things that aren't resolved in the family when you start working within a family foundation. You need to deal with the family dynamics and emotional issues. Using an outside facilitator can help you to try to identify and focus on the real issues—not whether Mom took you on more vacations or bought you more clothes or favored you over me or did or didn't do something that you haven't got over your anger about."

Donor-Consultants: Who Does What and for How Much?

Advice from philanthropy consultants covers a lot of territory. These days, financial services firms are expanding their advisory services to meet demand from affluent donors and aging boomers. You'll find philanthropic services consultants at virtually all the wealth-management companies, from Northern Trust to Bank of America and from Morgan Stanley to Fidelity and Citibank. Usually, at such companies, the advice is included in administrative and investment fees charged for managing your financial arrangements, whether donor-advised funds, stock portfolio, trust funds, or so on.

The process of evaluating a philanthropy consultant is the same as that of evaluating other key professionals in your life, from lawyers to doctors to money managers. Ask for references, and actually check them. Spend some time deciding whether the advisor "is a good communicator and responsive to your needs," says consultant and donor Tracy Gary. Take it slowly. You also want someone who has experience working with tax attorneys, estate planners, and accountants—"someone who knows the players," as one consultant puts it. Interview several to find the right fit.

Besides specialized advisors at financial services firms, there are a number of other choices. Here's a brief rundown.

♦ **Private consultants:** Generally, to make working with a dedicated private consultant worthwhile, you'll want at least $100,000 earmarked for giving. Private consultant fees vary widely. Depending on the kind of work, the location, and whether it's a sole proprietor or a national consultancy, the gamut runs from $100 per hour to $5,000 a day. Some charge a percentage of your total contributions, usually 3 percent to 5 percent.

"But there are nuances to this," explains consultant Lee Draper. "There are different advantages to having someone local or a firm with a breadth of capacity. It's about finding the appropriate skill sets." Just look before you leap.

Among the private services, the largest is likely Rockefeller Philanthropy Advisors (RPA) in New York. Originally the private philanthropy arm of the Rockefeller family, RPA reinvented itself in 2002 as an independent nonprofit philanthropy service for high–net worth families and well-heeled private foundations and corporations. It launched with a staff of fifteen, advising on annual grants of $30 million. By 2008, the staff had grown to thirty-five and the annual grants were $200 million. RPA provides philanthropy planning, administration, management, and advice, helping clients to, say, set up a foundation, identify organizations that meet their missions or intentions, and manage all grant-making operations.

In addition, with the rising interest in tackling worldwide problems such as the spread of AIDS or human trafficking, advisory services that can help donors with the complexities of effective cross-border giving are springing up. These advisors are not to be confused with the dozens of nonprofit groups and nongovernmental organizations (NGOs) that work around the world. Rather, donor advisory consulting firms, such as Arabella Philanthropic Investment Advisors, based in Washington, D.C.; Geneva Global, in Wayne, Pennsylvania; or Calvin Edwards, in Atlanta, Georgia, are for-profit services that work with families and corporations as well as government agencies and nonprofit foundations to plan, set up, and manage international philanthropic projects.

In theory, these services ease the path and deepen the impact for global giving by aggregating contributions and managing on-the-ground efforts with local smarts and oversight. However, most of them are still too young to evaluate. While the jury is out, your best approach to working with these for-profit advisors is a cautious one: Check references. Kick tires. Maintain vigilance.

Six Key Points for a Consultant Agreement Letter

Discuss these issues beforehand to make sure that you and the consultant share the same expectations. It's also a good idea, of course, to have an attorney review your contract. Your agreement letter ought to include the following:

1. A brief outline of the goals of your arrangement.

2. The details of how often you'll meet and what you plan to accomplish.

3. A description of the consultant's responsibilities.

4. The details on whether or not you expect written reports or presentations.

5. The timetable for the work.

6. The consultant's fees and a schedule of payment.

◆ **Nonprofit officers:** Planned-giving officers at nonprofit organizations, community foundations, and public institutions such as libraries, museums, and universities are available (and eager) to meet with potential donors. They can help you figure out how to best align your needs and wishes with giving options. For example, at the Minneapolis Foundation, one of the oldest and largest community foundations in the country, Gift-planning Officer Mary Ellis Peterson listens carefully to donors and offers advice about "different kinds of gifts and lots of ways to leverage interests." Such advice is free and, although there are expectations that you're interested in making some sort of donation, you're not liable to feel any pressure.

◆ **Peer mentors:** Launching or becoming a member of a giving circle (see Chapter 6) is a participatory and low-cost way to become educated about how you prefer to give and what makes for effective grant making. Getting involved in what are called "federated programs," such as the Red Cross, CARE, or the United Way—groups with national management entities and local branches—also provides a terrific way to learn from knowledgeable donors and experienced consultants. "If donors want to be more involved, federated programs educate people and make that perfectly possible," says Diana Aviv, CEO of Independent Sector.

Checklist for Assessing an Advisor

Philanthropist and consultant Tracy Gary, author of *Inspired Philanthropy*, devised this scorecard for evaluating an advisor. Rate the advisor's responses to your concerns on a scale of 1 to 5 (5 being your highest level of comfort). A score of 1 or 2 in seven or more categories ought to provoke serious reevaluation.

Advisor Response	My Comfort Level
Does the advisor reflect back your vision, goals, hopes, and dreams in such a way that you can recognize yourself in that "mirror"?	5 4 3 2 1
Does the advisor see what makes you unique?	5 4 3 2 1
Is the advisor compassionate and empathetic?	5 4 3 2 1
Does the advisor respond tactfully to sensitive personal information?	5 4 3 2 1
Do you feel a connection and a bond?	5 4 3 2 1
Is this someone in whom you feel comfortable confiding?	5 4 3 2 1
Does the advisor use plain English and help you understand the issues?	5 4 3 2 1
Does this person give you credit for your ideals, as well as your success?	5 4 3 2 1
Does this person get excited about the thought of helping you create plans that will express and pass on your values as well as money?	5 4 3 2 1

Does the advisor seem like a team player?	5 4 3 2 1
Does he or she listen as well as talk?	5 4 3 2 1
Does the advisor pick up on subtle cues from you and your partner or spouse? Or do you have to insist on important points over and over to get the point through?	5 4 3 2 1
Would you enjoy working with this person as a cocreator of your life and legacy plan?	5 4 3 2 1
Do you trust and respect this advisor?	5 4 3 2 1

Caveat Emptor When Choosing a Donor Consultant

Then there's the dark side of philanthropy consulting: Anyone can hang out a shingle as a philanthropy expert. There are neither credentials nor certifications required to back up the claim.

One group, the recently launched National Network of Consultants to Grantmakers (NNCG), is trying to amend that. Based in Los Angeles, the nonprofit organization has begun setting standards for performance and ethics for philanthropy consultants. NNCG vets its member consultants by evaluating their level of experience and client references. Thus far, in a small field, it has attracted a respectable few hundred members nationwide. Self-described as "part think-tank and part service organization," the group, according to

founding member consultant Lee Draper, is set up like, say,
the National Association of Personal Financial Advisors. The
idea is that membership in NNCG will signal trust and experience to donors. For full-fledged (rather than associate)
membership, a consultant must provide references from a
minimum of five grant makers who have been clients
during the preceding three years.

A Lucky Man: Michael J. Fox

Experts from other fields can also serve as philanthropy advisors. You may, for example, have targeted a research cause
but need help deciding where to focus or what to fund in
order to effect the change you envision. You may have
defined the mission but need ongoing advice about progress
in a field. Or you may want to coordinate efforts within a
wider community. In such cases, tapping the expertise of
outside advisors such as economists, scientists, anthropolo-
gists, teachers, psychiatrists, sculptors, musicians, and so on

can help you better determine where and how you can make a difference. One model for this kind of alliance, albeit on a highly progressive scale, is offered in the work being done by Michael J. Fox.

Actor and icon, husband and father, Fox has played many roles in his life. His latest, as American's leading activist for research into curing and treating Parkinson's disease, represents his greatest challenge. "The vast majority of us are pretty good people who want to help out," explains Fox. "You feel, 'Wow, I was really lucky to be able to do that!' You don't think, 'Wow, they were really lucky I was here.'"

By the time he was twenty-four, Fox had catapulted to fame and riches as the star of the television series *Family Ties* and the blockbuster movie *Back to the Future*. He was only thirty when the disease was diagnosed in 1991. Now in his late forties, Fox has spent years coping with Parkinson's—"a progressive, degenerative and incurable neurological disorder," as he puts it in his best-selling 2002 memoir *Lucky Man*. Despite Fox's illness, that choice of title reflects his philosophy of life.

"I don't want to be glib about it, because I know this is really hard for a lot of people, and it's hard for me physically, and emotionally sometimes," Fox acknowledges. "But it's become clear to me that I'm really lucky. The stuff I have— my wife, Tracy; my kids; my career; the experiences I've had; the effect I've had—I've gotten a lot, for one human being. The shaking and the not always being able to do what I want to do—it's not that bad. I don't feel anger; I don't feel fear. I have a full life. I don't look at the world through PD-colored glasses. I look at the world the way I've always looked at the world: I feel really lucky."

Fox's privileged circumstances have heightened his sense of obligation. "If I didn't work again, it would be okay, and that's huge. My situation is unique. I don't have to worry about health insurance or losing my job or the other big issues that most people with Parkinson's have to deal with. So it's freed me up to do this stuff."

"This stuff" is his typically self-deprecating way of describing the Michael J. Fox Foundation for Parkinson's Research, which he founded in 2000. Since then, the New York–based organization has raised and funded over $120 million in research. "I'm not so much a philanthropist as an encourager of philanthropy," he says.

Fox's private journey as a Parkinson's patient began to evolve into a public campaign in 1999, when he was asked to testify before Congress in support of increased funding for research into the disease. Because he was a star, he says, "there was all this attention." Recognizing the impact he could have, he found himself wrestling with a daunting question: "Don't I have a responsibility to do something about this, whether I want to or not?"

As Fox learned more about Parkinson's research, he was troubled by his growing awareness of unmet needs. "I met a lot of scientists who said, 'We're limited only by money and manpower. We know where we're going. We just need to be able to do it,'" Fox reports. "So I thought, 'What can I do?' Public visibility is like currency, and in order not to devalue it, I needed to be careful about how I spent it. I can raise money for research, but where's it going to go? I realized that I needed to design something that seeks out the best places to put funding, because if people are going to give money through me, then I have a real responsibility to know where every penny goes and to have the last word on the organization that funnels it." From the outset, Fox was driven by realizing what wasn't being accomplished anywhere else. "There were big institutions that were covering big things, like the National Institutes of Health, but we wanted to speed up the review process and to reward risk," he explains. "I wanted to take an entrepreneurial approach, to look at it like a start-up. It seemed to me that to catch the stuff that was falling through the cracks, what was needed was a Navy SEAL–type thing—an extremely narrowly focused, guerrilla-warfare, ad hoc research group. We could be specific about it and say, 'We want to create a dopaminergic cell line'—a line of stem cells that create dopamine— or 'We want to work on identifying Parkinson's through biomarkers.'"

In addition to funding research, another priority for the foundation is "convening—getting people together," as Fox puts it. "We host and run 15 to 20 scientific meetings a year," says Deborah Brooks, president and CEO of the foundation. Its goals reflect Fox's sense of urgency; the foundation promotes research designed to get results that can have an impact on patients faster than generally happens within large bureaucracies.

Fox was particularly dismayed by President Bush's 2001 decision to allow federal funding for research only on stem-cell lines that had already been extracted from embryos—a compromise that imposed severe limitations on future research. "I know I'm not the first Mr. Smith to go to Washington and get worked up, but the biggest frustration was coming face-to-face with political expediency," Fox says. "On the issue of funding, politicians aren't rewarded for far-sightedness. There's no political upside to that; it won't result in votes for them. An issue like stem cells can bite you on the ass, so you see the deals being made to satisfy a certain part of the constituency. And as a result, something that's potentially so important and groundbreaking and paradigm-shifting becomes a chip in the game."

However, Fox remains resolutely upbeat. "I do think in terms of a cure," he admits. "In the bliss of not being a scientist, I can look at things simplistically. We're not there yet, but we've made a lot of progress. Our understanding of things is growing exponentially. However far we have to go, I do believe this stuff is going to happen in our lifetime."

Fox Learned Some Tips Along the Way

For those interested in creating foundations or other charitable institutions, Fox offers three pointers for staying focused and reaching charitable goals.

1. "Be really specific about what you want to do," he advises. "If we had one foot in the advocacy pond and one in caregiving and one in research, we'd never get anywhere."

2. "Find people you can trust. I have no management skills, but I realized I only had to be smart enough to find people who are smarter than me and keep them close."

3. "Always be pure in motive—and completely transparent."

How to Choose and Work with Wealth Managers

While the focus here is on working with donor consultants, you will, of course, also need the expertise and advice of wealth managers and investment counselors to develop a comfortable and consistent giving plan. When working with any financial pro, from wealth managers and investment counselors to tax accountants and estate attorneys, the overarching imperative is, do not give up control. Make sure your money and investments are working for you, not the other way around. Here are key ways to keep money managers on track.

♦ Be clear about your expectations. If your advisor doesn't provide satisfactory answers to your questions or can't translate terminology about market metrics, he or she might be a bad fit. Don't assume that's the way it's supposed to be. Request a course correction, or shop for another advisor. To find one, ask for referrals from friends and associates. Seek recommendations from an expert you already trust, whether your lawyer or your accountant. Interview several advisors to check rapport, then ask for references.

♦ Keep the big picture in focus. Don't get bogged down in the latest digital tools or trends. You want to see—and understand—your entire life and goals on one piece of paper. When advisors suggest changes or adjustments, ask about later outcomes and how those will meet your goals.

♦ Be clear about your tolerance for risk. And make sure the advisor honors it. That means you're aware of what kinds of investments are being made with your money and how well (or not) they are performing.

♦ Keep tabs on performance. Check rates of returns and asset allocation strategies, advises financial planner Marjorie Beutel, at the New York–based Beutel & Joyce. "You ought to know how your investments performed against the market." If you switch advisors or aggregate assets from another firm, make sure there's a transition strategy that's thought-out and tax efficient. You don't want to immediately cash out everything. It'll likely cost you big-time.

♦ Understand fees and communications. Find out how much is charged to service your particular account (fees tend to vary with how much money is under management). Ask for a breakdown that details management fees or whether fees equal a percentage of assets. Check commissions, product fees, load or performance fees, and the like. Identify who at the firm will take care of your requests and needs, from wire transfers to questions about statements. Discuss when meetings will be held—quarterly or annually?

♦ Don't become passive. Schedule regular meetings, and don't let a partner or spouse handle them alone. Get involved. You don't want to suffer a crisis and have no personal relationship with your portfolio manager.

Don't Settle for a So-So Advisor

Horrific events don't always happen to someone else. Jennifer Caprile knows this all too vividly. In 2002, when she was only twenty-seven, her husband was killed in a car accident near their San Diego home. In the terrible aftermath, Caprile received several million dollars from a life insurance policy and a lawsuit settlement. "Our life was about struggling to buy a home and moving forward," she says. "All of a sudden I had a lot money, and survivor's guilt. I spent a long time being uncomfortable with the money."

Caprile kept working as a flight attendant until 2006, though she no longer needed the income. "It gave me some stability," she explains. She also had to come to terms with her bitter fortune. "I spent the first few years splurging, just to get rid of the money that I didn't think I deserved. I'd unconsciously do things spur of the moment, like go to Hawaii."

Women frequently go on spending binges after being widowed or divorced. Reality takes time to set in. Most advisors recommend waiting at least a year to make any serious financial decisions, including what to do about your home, assuming you can afford to wait.

In due course, Caprile met with several male financial planners to sort out an investment strategy. "I would tell them what was happening and they'd say 'yeah, yeah, yeah,' and 'you should invest in this and this mutual fund,' and 'you should be interested in these bonds.' I felt like they were giving me a generic spiel. They weren't listening."

Eventually, the young widow found her way to Candace Bahr, a wealth manager who runs the Bahr Investment Group, in the San Diego area, and who is also cofounder of the nonprofit Women's Institute for Financial Education. "Candace listened for two hours, asking questions like how I saw myself in five or ten years," says Caprile. "I felt like she was taking the time to recommend unique investment strategies rather than rolling me in with the rest of her clients."

Still healing, Caprile, now in her mid-thirties, has resettled in Los Angeles and begun philanthropic work in Africa and Vietnam. Her experience of being frustrated with advisors is a common one. One recent study by the Wharton Business School for State Street Global Advisors found that a whopping 70 percent of clients reported that their advisors had never asked how they might improve the client-advisor relationship. "Women specifically have issues at major brokerage firms," says Bahr. "A lot of what we need to do is listen, and many people in the industry aren't trained to do that. They're trained to give solutions as quickly as possible and go on to next person."

Chapter 9

WHAT COMES NEXT?

GETTING MORE INVOLVED

Once people step onto the path of giving, involvement tends to deepen over time and the rewards of the journey truly begin.

Jewelle Bickford, for example, a senior advisor at the Rothschild Group investment-banking firm, has contributed to charities for years. A fairly engaged donor, she was invited to join the boards of Randolph Macon College and the Trisha Brown Dance Company. But in 2007, Bickford traveled around Rwanda and found the experience gut-wrenching and eye-opening. Back home in New York, she became involved with Women for Women International, a Washington, D.C.–based organization that aids women around the world who are victims of war. "It changes your life," says Bickford. "Nothing has affected me like this."

Nowadays, Bickford has joined the board of Women for

Women and is shedding her other charitable commitments. "One woman can make a difference," she says.

Choosing a Higher Profile

That motivation to move forward, to dig in rather than look on, flows from the fulfillment that giving brings. "Philanthropy helps to clarify what you care about, because you can't do everything," says New York social activist Barbara Dobkin, who has donated millions of dollars to causes that support women, the Jewish community, and social justice. "It prioritizes your values."

And what tends to follow is stepping into the limelight, as donors realize that when giving is more visible, it's often also more effective. After years of preferring to donate anonymously, Dobkin has recently become more public about both her contributions and her beliefs. She is founding chair of the board of directors at the Jewish Women's Archive, founder and chair of Ma'yan: The Jewish Women's Project of the Jewish Community Center in Manhattan, and chair of the board of the Hadassah Foundation. She also serves on the boards of Advancing Women Professionals and the Jewish Community, the White House Project, *Lilith* magazine, and the Women's Funding Network.

"You have to come to terms not only with the money but also with getting comfortable being out there," says Dobkin about taking on a leadership role. "I found out that if you're not out there, people assume you're not doing it. They read

"Giving makes you feel good," says billionaire Sandy Weill, retired chairman of Citigroup and now full-time philanthropist. If you're waiting for later or a better time, Weill has more advice: "Shrouds don't have pockets."

or learn who's on a board and who donates, and that influences decisions. A lot of giving is social."

You can boost your investment in giving in many ways, of course. You can start your own charity, structure an individual giving program, join a nonprofit board, increase your contributions of time or money, become a fund-raiser for your chosen charity, or even switch to a nonprofit career.

Anthony Kennedy Shriver: Advocate for the Power of One

Despite there being so much dire need in the world, one person with one idea truly can improve the lives of many. "Public service is really an addictive profession," says Anthony Kennedy Shriver, who comes from a family that knows a thing or two about serving others. "It allows you to come home from the office every day and feel great about yourself, because what you've done means something to another human being."

His uncles were President John F. Kennedy and Senator Robert F. Kennedy. His dad, Sargent Shriver, was the first director of the Peace Corps. So in 1988, after graduating from Georgetown University, Anthony Kennedy Shriver had his pick of privileged paths. "In the back of my mind I figured I'd study for the LSATs in the fall and head for law school," he says.

But over that summer break, Shriver decided to travel around to look into state funding for a small organization he had formed at Georgetown. The group, called Best Buddies, fostered one-to-one friendships between students and people with intellectual disabilities. It had produced unexpectedly strong bonds and benefits for all involved.

Shriver credits his childhood relationship with his aunt Rosemary Kennedy, who had an intellectual disability, for giving him an appreciation of the talents of people with disabilities like hers. "I used to think how disabled she was, how she couldn't eat by herself or get dressed or get a job or do anything you need to do to be considered successful in America," he recalls. "Then one day she jumped in the pool and she could swim better than anyone in the family. Every person has a skill set."

If his aunt was a guiding spirit—and later in her life she spent two months every winter with Shriver and his family—then it was his mother who was the source of the actual model. Shriver got the idea for Best Buddies from attending the Special Olympics (SO), the international athletic competition for people with intellectual disabilities, founded by Eunice Kennedy Shriver. At SO events on campuses, he noted that the participating athletes seemed to feel and perform better when local students looked after them. Afterward, on their own, the athletes had a more difficult time. Back at Georgetown, Shriver set up the Best Buddies program, which assessed needs and personalities and then matched participating students with friends with disabilities.

He never did make it to law school. "I met some people on the state level in Tallahassee who offered to provide funding for the program statewide, and that's how I wound up in Miami," says Shriver. "There was an amazing vacuum in public service at the college level at that time. Students at different schools would hear what a great experience Best Buddies was and want to form a chapter. I never had a plan. It took on a life of its own."

Working fifteen-hour days and leveraging those trademark Kennedy qualities—the unfailing courtesy and charm, the high-level access, the charismatic grin, those cheekbones—Shriver has built Best Buddies into a worldwide nonprofit with programs in all fifty states and more than twenty countries. The mission has also expanded to include advancing employment opportunities, in addition to friendships, for people with intellectual disabilities. High-profile fund raisers, some attended by supporters like Shriver's sister, Maria Shriver Schwarzenegger, California's first lady, help fuel growth. In 2006, Best Buddies had assets of more than $4 million and served 350,000 individuals, while contributing community services worth more than $70 million.

"I'd like to go beyond friendships and jobs and move into housing," says Shriver, who's now in his mid-forties. He and his wife, Alina, a Cuban-born former ballerina, have four kids. Just about everyone in the family has a Best Buddy. "Most of the problems fade when one human being gets to know someone and can develop a sensitivity to that person," says Shriver. "So in twenty years, I hope I won't have to be doing this, because people will find out what people with intellectual disabilities can offer without getting matched up or filling out forms."

Forming a Nonprofit Corporation

If you decide to launch your own charity, there are step-by-step rules to forming a nonprofit corporation in compliance with local, state, and federal laws. This overview comes from the Citizen Media Law Project, a partnership of Harvard Law School's Berkman Center for Internet & Society and the Center for Citizen Media (see citmedialaw.org).

Step 1. Draft your mission. Take the time to write out a mission statement that identifies the societal need you wish to satisfy and how your nonprofit corporation will go about it. Also figure out a fund raising plan and your annual budget.

Step 2. Incorporate your nonprofit. Most small nonprofit organizations incorporate in the state where they operate. Get in touch with your secretary of state and request all the needed forms. Although you are not required to do so, consider registering your business name as a federal and/or state trademark.

Step 3. Get your Employer Identification Number. You can apply for an EIN with Form SS-4 at the IRS Web site (irs.gov) or by calling 800-829-4933.

Step 4. Apply for tax exemptions. You must apply for federal income tax exemptions before being able to enjoy state and local tax exemptions.

Next steps:
- Register with your state's attorney general.
- Open a bank account for your business.
- Obtain any required local licenses or permits.
- Apply for a nonprofit postal permit.
- Obtain appropriate insurance.

How Nonprofit Committees
and Boards Work

Typically, volunteers and donors looking for greater hands-on involvement join an organization's committee or board. As in the corporate world, committees form the basic structure of nonprofit boards and address a gamut of organizational issues and activities pertinent to the group and its resources. Most of the time, you'll find committees for financial oversight, fund-raising, governance or legal compliance, executive management, and development or programs. After that, there are any number of advisory councils and committees that launch for various short-term or ongoing challenges.

Generally, board trustees act as stewards of the organization's charitable mission and watchdogs for its performance and ethics. Board members of a public charity (rather than a private or family foundation) hire and fire executive directors or chief executives, review performance, and ensure that the organization fulfills its obligations. The board also gets involved in strategic planning, management succession, policy-making, and setting financial, budget-related, and other goals, say, by creating a five-year plan. As a board member, you're expected to be enthusiastic and engaged. By joining, you're signaling that you want to work for the organization's growth and success, whether by helping with fund-raising or by contributing skills, money, or other resources.

Unlike in the corporate world, though, nonprofit board members or trustees are frequently unpaid volunteers. As a result, the challenge of finding people willing to devote time and energy to such service has, in the past, led trustees to recruit friends and professional associates. That, in turn, often led to board conflicts of interest and less-than-competent directors. Today, along with a host of other improvements in accountability, larger nonprofits are actively addressing cronyism and similar issues and making serious efforts to appoint only qualified board members.

Similarly, smaller charities and families are increasingly looking for outside perspectives to help govern private foundations. Board members are tapping their advisors at wealth-management firms and independent philanthropy consultants to act as active board members. "As we govern organizations in the future, it will be interesting to see what the future board looks like," says fund-raising consultant Marnie Maxwell, referring to current efforts to improve the expertise and diversity of members.

Diane von Furstenberg Decides to Join a Board—Fast

Increasingly, when a cause or group hits the right nerve people are responding quickly and becoming directly engaged. Diane von Furstenberg fits that bill. Like many American women lately, she has stepped up to help improve the safety and survival of women everywhere.

In addition to being chief executive of her own global fashion business, the veteran designer is also a mother and grandmother, the wife of media mogul Barry Diller, a creator with her husband of the Diller–von Furstenberg Family Foundation, and president of the trade group the Council of Fashion Designers of America. So it's all the more compelling that within weeks of attending a fall 2007 luncheon for an organization called Vital Voices Global Partnership that the designer decided to join its board. "Vital Voices resonates the most for me because it embraces all the things I believe in and stand for," says von Furstenberg. "That's why I want to be more involved."

Initiated in 1997 by then first lady Hillary Clinton and secretary of state Madeleine Albright after they had attended the United Nations Fourth World Conference on Women, in Beijing, Vital Voices supports women community leaders worldwide. The group has attracted support from women of all political stripes—from actress Sally Field to former Hewlett-Packard CEO Carly Fiorina to Texas Republican senator Kay Bailey Hutchison.

Besides acting as a spokeswoman, von Furstenberg has helped design the Vital Voices logo, created some of its marketing material, and, of course, become involved in board management and planning.

What You Should Know Before
You Join a Board

Being invited to join a nonprofit board or governance committee is certainly flattering and generally rewarding. But board work is also time-consuming and challenging. Before making a commitment, it's critical to learn, first, whether the board deserves your investment and, second, whether the skills and resources you bring match its current needs.

Make sure you're well educated about the organization and clearly understand what's expected of you and what the group plans going forward, both short and long term. You'll want to review the nonprofit's background and financial standing. Ask to see the certificate of incorporation; application for federal income tax exemption; and, perhaps, recent board agendas and minutes, to get an idea of the board's concerns and accomplishments. You'll also want to evaluate the latest annual report, financial statements, and marketing material, including any media-outreach efforts. A chat with current board members and the organization's chief executive will reveal a good deal about members' responsibilities and backgrounds.

If you expect to serve for a few years or more, you'll want to delve a bit deeper. In that case, nonprofit governance group BoardSource, based in Washington D.C., suggests you review the following key areas before making your decision:

♦ The programs: Ask about the organization's mission, how its current programs relate to that mission, and whether you can visit any programs to see for yourself how the group works. You'll also want to ask about the organization's strategic plan.

♦ The finances: Of course, you'll want to check the group's audited statements and income/outgo to make sure it's on a sound financial footing. In addition, does the board discuss and approve the annual budget? Will you be receiving regular financial reports?

◆ The clients or constituencies: Find out which constituents the organization serves and whether these groups are satisfied.

◆ The board's structure: How many members and committees are there? Are the responsibilities of the board as a whole, its individual members, and the various committees clear and thought-out? Has the board put checks and balances in place to prevent conflicts of interest? Check into directors' and officers' liability coverage (described below).

◆ Individual responsibilities: Have you defined the ways you can contribute? Are you prepared for the time and resources expected of you? If you need any training or education, can the board provide that? What about fundraising? Are you expected to solicit friends, family, or associates or contribute a specified amount?

◆ The board's relationship to staff: How does everyone get along? Is the board satisfied with the performance of the executive staff?

Moving from Wish to Fulfillment

Launched by the Ford Foundation in 2001, the GrantCraft project works to promote grant-making lessons in philanthropy for foundations and funders. This GrantCraft chart illustrates how six funders started with an idea, articulated a theory to accomplish the change they envisioned, and ended with a program model for making grants to individuals. (The fund names are changed, but descriptions are based on real programs.)

	Purpose	Theory	Program
For All You've Done Prizes	To offer thanks and support to accomplished community leaders, artists, and innovators	A prize validates an individual's work, makes way for continued achievement, and inspires others to excellence	Make unrestricted awards to accomplished individuals
Leading Edge Fellowships	To develop a pipeline of leaders with new solutions to social problems	Ideas for social change develop best among individuals working outside institutional constraints	Provide fellowships to social entrepreneurs and promote networking for mutual support
Saving Today's Einstein Grants	To enable scholars under threat of death or other serious harm to continue their work in safety	Individuals, not institutions, face threats and need safe haven to continue their work	Offer grant support and institutional connections to enable threatened scholars to continue their work in safe countries
Crossing Boundaries Health Research Grants	To promote a high-performing health care system and increase the quality of care for vulnerable populations	Working internationally and across disciplines, individuals can learn what works and transfer effective practices	Support mid-career health care professionals from abroad to work for a year in the U.S. on policy-oriented research

(continued on next page)

	Purpose	Theory	Program
Home-Grown Achievers Scholarships	To strengthen the ability of public universities to compete for the top high school seniors in their states	Linking top students with public universities will strengthen the educational system and keep the most talented students in the state	Give full-tuition scholarships to 20 high school seniors each year, to be used at any of the state's public universities
Equity in Arts Leadership Internships	To cultivate and diversify the next generation of museum and arts organization leaders	Giving a diverse group of under-graduates exposure to arts organizations will inspire them to enjoy the arts and perhaps pursue careers in the field	Provide funding to students and organi-zations to support 150 internships per year

There Are Risks to Being a
Board Member

Such service also carries some legal and financial risks, which vary depending on your state's regulations or law. As a safeguard, check the nonprofit's liability-insurance coverage. Smaller groups in particular may carry general liability insurance but lack a directors' and officers' liability (D&O) policy. D&O policies indemnify individual board members against actual or alleged acts or decisions that general liability policies don't usually cover, such as employee embezzlement, unfair hiring practices, harassment suits, and other issues, advises Marguerite Griffin, national director of philanthropic services at Northern Trust.

If you join the board of a group that lacks D&O coverage, you may want to recommend that it be purchased. A typical policy with coverage limits of $1 million has varying deductibles and starts at about $700 in annual premiums. In a pinch, says Griffin, "you may be able to get D&O coverage as a rider to your homeowner's insurance policy. Check with your carrier." For details about affordable directors' and officers' liability policies, a good source is the Association of Small Foundations (202-580-6560; smallfoundations.org).

Family Foundations and the 5 Percent Payout Controversy

One big idea for increasing the country's charitable engagement and resources raises the issue of the intensifying debate around the so-called 5 percent payout rule for family and private foundations.

That is, no matter how many millions of dollars in assets a family foundation has, by law, trustees need disburse only 5 percent of that foundation's assets each year to charity to qualify for tax write-offs. And a part of that percentage is allowed for administrative and staff costs. As a result, many foundations are giving only 3 percent or so to good works. (The foundation may distribute more than 5 percent in grants, of course, just no less.)

In recent years, as the nonprofit sector comes under greater congressional and media scrutiny, a growing group of social activists and some legislators have begun to argue that, in order for a foundation to rate any tax benefit, the 5 percent annual payout rate should be raised to 6 percent, or even more.

"When the donors established their foundations, they received a significant tax benefit, depriving the country of tax revenues," says Lynn Korda Kroll, a longtime volunteer and donor, as well as vice-chairperson of the UJA Federation of New York and president of Women's Philanthropy at the UJA. "Having received that benefit, it seems to me that they are morally and ethically bound to disburse those funds, perhaps more than the legally mandated 5 percent, to worthy charitable institutions. Otherwise the only ones benefiting are the wealthy donors who have saved on taxes."

What's more, most private foundations are structured to exist in perpetuity. So while the mission and intent of an original founder several generations ago might have been "to help the poor" or "to find a cure for cancer," existing trustees are often more focused on growing the endowment. The mission, or what's called "donor intent," gets lost in the management.

The flip side of this argument is that by spending more now, foundations will pay down their principal and thus diminish not only the foundation's long-term earnings but, ultimately, its impact. Similarly, during times when assets lose value, such as when the stock market cratered late in 2008, many foundation owners express concern about even paying out the 5 percent minimum.

Kroll, for one, acknowledges that but points to the greater moral obligation. "Particularly during economically difficult times, when government funding is cut to important programs and institutions, the money in private foundations could be of great use."

If you operate a family foundation or are establishing one, consider the benefits of stepping past the 5 percent payout rule.

So You're Thinking About an "Encore Career"

Working for the social good can provide a lot more payback than working for a paycheck, especially for the increasing numbers of aging professionals who are shifting into the next phase of their careers.

This issue—just what the 78 million baby boomers will do after they reach traditional retirement age—was investigated in a 2008 survey of 3,500 people between the ages of forty-four and seventy. Sponsored by Civic Ventures, in San Francisco, which performs research on work and aging, and the MetLife Foundation, in New York, it's billed as the first national survey to look into the appeal of second careers that work for social benefits.

Already, according to the survey, about 6 percent of Americans in that age group, or 5.3 million, are working in so-called encore careers—defined as "positions that combine income and personal meaning with social impact." More significantly, the survey found that 84 percent of those currently working in encore careers report great satisfaction. And 94 percent say they see positive results from their work and know they're making a difference.

This trend is likely to mushroom as more boomers move into their fifties and sixties and look for both purposeful work and continued income. The survey found that a majority of Americans aged forty-four to seventy want to use their skills and experience to help others. In addition, the youngest respondents tend to be most interested in social-purpose careers; fully 50 percent of boomers aged forty-five to fifty say they want to join the 7 percent of their group already engaged in such careers.

What You Need to Know
to Transition

While it is certainly possible to jump from the for-profit world into the nonprofit sector, the transition is not always as easy as you might think.

Nonprofits prefer to hire people with direct knowledge of and experience in the sector, much like any other industry. The organizations have learned the hard way that for-profit measures of success, like quarterly sales goals or revenue targets, don't always translate into success in the charitable world.

New York–based nonprofit recruiter Virginia Strull notes, "For-profit professionals looking to make the jump can be arrogant." When for-profit pros are willing to take a salary

Online Job Listings of Nonprofit Positions

- ASAE & the Center for Association Leadership (asaecenter.org)
- The *Chronicle of Higher Education* (chronicle.com)
- The *Chronicle of Philanthropy* (philanthropy.com)
- Community Career Center (nonprofitjobs.org)
- Council on Foundations (cof.org)
- Dot Org Jobs (dotorgjobs.com)
- The Foundation Center (foundationcenter.org)
- Idealist.org
- IndependentSector.org
- NonProfitCareer.com
- The *Nonprofit Times* (nptimes.com)

cut or join a bunch of "do-gooders," they figure all they have to do is show up. "They assume nonprofit work is easy," says Strull, who is also president of Women in Development (WID), a membership network for women in the field. "But program directors, for instance, tend to be highly educated, and have built a client base. Most nonprofits need specialized staff in their particular field. In fact, most people in nonprofits are overly qualified."

Yet at the same time, the generation of boomer nonprofit executives will also be retiring. That trend, plus the overall growth of the sector, is likely to yield new opportunities for business-trained professionals to jump ladders.

If you are thinking about a transition, Strull suggests you learn about the nonprofit sector beforehand. "Lawyers wouldn't dare to write a contract without taking a law contracts class," she says. "Similarly, professionals who want to move into nonprofit work need to sign up for some training to gain some general knowledge." For instance, she advises, "they need to know what a board does, to understand what a major gifts officer does, to understand strategies for governance and so on. They need to know the theory, practice and vocabulary of fund-raising and how it's structured, before plunging into it."

Increasingly, as more people turn their interest to philanthropy, there are inexpensive training outlets for nonprofit work. Check the online or in-class course offerings at the Foundation Center, which is headquartered in New York and operates offices in Atlanta, Cleveland, San Francisco, and Washington, D.C. Plus, education- and career-development

Training for Nonprofit Pros

The IRS offers several free online courses to help you develop professional skills for nonprofit management and governance. Most take thirty minutes. Visit StayExempt.org to check out its e-learning modules on applying for tax-exempt status, understanding employment issues, filing Form 990s, and more.

In addition, more than 250 colleges and universities around the country now offer individual courses on and programs that award certificates and degrees in nonprofit management, fund-raising, and similar subjects. The Indianapolis-based Center on Philanthropy, for instance, offers a course called "Purposeful Boards, Powerful Fundraising."

audio conferences are offered by the Association of Fundraising Professionals.

Raising the Bar on Fund-Raising Practices

Over the past decade or so, federal, state, and local authorities have all stepped up their efforts to regulate charitable solicitations. Watchdogs such as Charity Navigator and the BBB Wise Giving Alliance offer consumers a wealth of vetted information that can inform their decisions about contributions. Simultaneously, nonprofits are busy becoming more transparent and ethical in their fund-raising practices. The dishonest solicitation and widespread scams of the recent past have diminished.

If you want to become involved in raising money for charities, take some time to review the donor bill of rights and best-practice seminars currently being developed by many of the field's associations and networking groups. Independent Sector, for instance, has been a leader in this area. According to its principles for responsible fund-raising, charities must develop procedures for appropriately acknowledging donor gifts and refusing gifts from donors with unethical or illegal motivations.

For guidelines and practical tips, also take a look at "How to Succeed in Fundraising by *Really* Trying," a booklet by noted philanthropist Lewis B. Cullman. As Cullman explains in the introduction, "Many years of fundraising and many missteps have brought me to a place where I can speak with confidence about raising money."

Cullman began building his fortune by orchestrating the country's first leveraged buyout, in 1964, with just $1,000. Subsequent deals led to his acquisition of a desk-calendar company and the "At-A-Glance" line of appointment books. He sold that company in 1999, and, along with his wife, Dorothy, dedicated his time to giving away most of his money.

"The most important thing you can do is try to leverage your gift when you're fundraising, because no matter how much you have, you never have enough," says Cullman. "I've done all kinds of matching and drop-dead challenges to raise funds for charities." His guide is divided into three sections: "Defining the Campaign," "Tools & Techniques," and "The Ask." It can be downloaded for free from LewisCullman.com.

Reengineering the Gala

The organizations that achieve success today put time and resources into making fund-raising events meaningful. They work at building relationships, and they've added diversity to their staff and public face. And although many charities, large and small, still rely on annual galas, these, too, have changed—they've become less formal.

Love 'em or hate 'em, and most people admit to both, big fund-raising parties remain the most popular way for charities to raise money. A typical charity fund-raiser reels in

$1 million, on average, says Los Angeles–based event planner Judith Levy, who has organized glamorous benefits for the movie studios as well as for national groups such as the Elisabeth Glaser Pediatric AIDS Foundation.

It's hard to find anyone who will admit to *wanting* to attend a big charity ball. "It's always a favor for a favor," says philanthropist Abby Disney. "You go to mine and I'll go to yours." Yet you also won't find a soul who believes a non-profit could raise equal money without one. Recently, one group decided to dispense with the cost and snooze factor of a benefit party and simply directly ask for donations. The upshot: one-third less funding for the year. No one can offer a good explanation for this, either—except that people like parties, the networking, the dressing up, and the seeing and being seen.

America's A-List Gala

The philanthropy world's killer gala has been the annual bash thrown by the Robin Hood Foundation, which has raised unimaginable amounts of money each year. An innovative venture-philanthropy organization that invests money and professional skills in battling poverty in New York City, Robin Hood donates 100 percent of contributions to programs. How? By asking its wealthy board members and friendly stakeholders to pick up the tab on administrative costs. Until recently, with enviable and elite donors and board members, including movie stars and Wall Street moguls, the Robin Hood benefit has started well ahead of the fund-raising curve. Still, the gala's secret weapon has been marketing-and-communications director Laurie Fabiano, a canny and experienced event planner.

"In 1999, when I arrived, the event was already successful, pulling in $3 to $6 million," says Fabiano. "It was held at the New York Armory, a standard event venue, and accommodated the standard 1,600 people." She decided to give the party a boost, and that has paid off big-time.

Fabiano moved the gala from the Armory to New York's cavernous Jacob Javits Center, an exhibition hall big enough for a three-ring circus. By 2006, the party had attracted $46 million in donations. In 2008, the charity event racked up an astounding $71 million, or 35 percent of the foundation's annual fund-raising revenue. Tables of ten sold for $30,000 to $250,000 a piece, depending on location—and 4,100 people sat at them. Fabiano's costs ran about $5 million. She says it's all about planning and knowing people who will really sell tickets to friends and colleagues.

Here are Laurie Fabiano's top-ten dos and don'ts for a successful gala:

1. Make it fun. That means *not* black tie.

2. Don't be predictable. "If you can't tell this event from last year's, people will start to hate it."

3. Provide great entertainment and spirit in the room.

4. Don't try to make a huge space "pretty." Be bold in your design and decorations.

5. Get the right people involved. You want names that will attract the demographic you're inviting, not glittery celebs to impress the media. Gala tickets aren't sold by the press.

6. Maximize resources. If one donor buys a table for ten, make sure you get contact information for the other nine.

7. Don't use the event to cultivate donors directly. There are other opportunities for that year-round.

8. But do use the event to get acquainted with people outside your donor circle.

9. Follow up. Most nonprofits don't contact attendees afterward.

10. Don't throw a gala as an excuse. Make sure that the event is the best way to reach your fund-raising goal and that you wouldn't be better served by putting energy and resources into tapping major donors or corporate partnerships. Many board members feel more comfortable selling a ticket to a party than asking a friend for money.

FINDING THE LEVER

"I'm an enormous believer in one person being able to change the world. In my own family, all around me, people have been driving movements to change the world. Sometimes you think it has to be some big important thing, but what matters is that you change one life."
—ANTHONY KENNEDY SHRIVER, FOUNDER, BEST BUDDIES

Chapter 10

WHAT'S YOUR LEGACY?

ENGAGING THE KIDS

The wealth in the country today, much of it first generation—money earned, not inherited—is without precedent. In 2007, the number of households with a net worth of $5 million or more hit 1.2 million, passing the million mark for the first time, according to a survey by Spectrem Group, a Chicago-based market researcher that tracks America's high–net worth profile. That's four times the number of a decade ago. Households worth $1 million jumped to 9.2 million—those figures exclude the value of primary residences, too.

Certainly, that acceleration in wealth has slowed. The number of $5 million households spiked 23 percent from 2005 to 2006, while the increase was a relatively flat 2 percent from 2006 to 2007. The coming few years, no doubt, will evidence a much different cycle. Even so, we're looking at record numbers of wealthy families.

Increasingly, as a result, the millions of new million-aires—largely boomers who earned their money the hard way—are wrestling with how to nurture their children's empathy and work ethic, especially at the upper echelons, where their children may be growing up with an elite sense of entitlement. "Money has become a challenge for many families," says Boston-based philanthropy consultant Ellen Remmer, who works with wealthy families. "A lot of people didn't grow up with money, and now they have more than they ever thought they would," she says. "They may be into status and buying toys and houses, while their kids are concerned with identity struggles."

Families with inherited wealth also face these and other challenges. "What I see among inheritors are people very locked up and afraid to make a move in any direction," says Sam Stegeman, who grew up in a wealthy Delaware family. "They have money but feel they can't talk about it." Now in his mid-thirties, Stegeman works with a group called Resource Generation, based in New York, and similar non-profit networks that help educate well-heeled donors under the age of forty about philanthropy. Stegeman says he wants to "help people to see money as a form of energy that can be used in a positive direction." As he puts it, "It's better to do work that averts an environmental crisis than to donate money for a cleanup."

The Challenges of Prosperity
for Kids

More and more often, such issues are persuading affluent parents—and mothers in particular—to bring families into meetings to talk about fears, to share stories, to become educated, and to listen to advice. "In the last few years, I've been approached by many more women looking to take the journey of helping their families focus on the range of resources," says New York–based trust and estate advisor Patricia Angus, whose clients are high–net worth families and family businesses. "They want to understand their family values and mission. This isn't transactional. They've done the estate planning. Now they're trying to prepare the next generation to have discussions about money and to understand the basics of financial education."

Even so, teaching kids about financial values and the lessons of giving has little to do with how much wealth the family controls.

Leadership Lessons via Penny
Philanthropy

In 1991, Teddy Gross, a New York playwright, was walking down the street with his daughter Nora, then three. Although Manhattan's avenues never lack for the needy, that day one homeless man in particular impressed the toddler. She asked her dad if they could take him home.

Because of that thorny question—and haven't all our kids asked similar questions at some point in our parenting lives?—he and Nora cofounded Common Cents. The organization makes a "perfect match between two of society's smallest denominators, pennies and children," says Gross.

Managed in partnership with New York City public schools, the Common Cents Penny Harvest now involves thousands of children each year and has become the largest child-philanthropy program in the United States. Deceptively simple in concept, the lessons of Harvest are both complex and lifelong. Kids between the ages of four and fourteen collect pennies. When they reach a set goal, working together, those who join the program's philanthropy roundtables decide how and where to donate the money. Three-quarters of the participating kids come from homes below the poverty level. "We are not educating people about philanthropy," clarifies Gross. "We are using philanthropy to educate kids."

Along the way, Gross has learned a thing or two himself about youngsters' ability to reach out to others. "People don't quite realize how much children are aware of—you have to ask them," he says. "Teachers and adults don't often start conversations about giving with kids, and they're usually surprised at what children observe. Empathy is profoundly powerful at the earliest ages. A two-year-old begins crying when another child cries, but, of course, that goes away as we differentiate from others."

In the 2006 school year, 770 New York City schools took part in the Penny Harvest, collecting a staggering 185 tons of pennies, or $655,508.54. More than 7,000 children sitting on 521 philanthropy roundtables made 1,283 monetary grants to nonprofits such as women's shelters, animal rights organizations, community gardens, and senior centers.

Model the Behavior You Want to See

With more or fewer zeros to their credit, and because success seems to be everywhere calibrated in dollars, families across the country are taking on similar issues. "The culture speaks with a boom. The sound of parents is much softer," says Joline Godfrey, whose Santa Barbara company Independent Means provides financial-education programs for youngsters.

As with all parenting, the effective way to shape children's habits is to model the behavior you'd like to see. For example, Godfrey recently got a call from a potential client in Los Angeles, a mother who had gathered a group of ten families whose daughters were graduating from a private high school. Could Godfrey set up a half-day retreat to teach the girls some basics about budgeting, credit cards, and the like, to prepare them for college? And how much would Godfrey charge for that? Godfrey figured she'd run the seminar for $5,000—$500 per graduate. The mother was shocked. "She said that was way too expensive and she couldn't possibly consider it," says Godfrey. After a few beats, she adds, "I'm sure each family spent three times that much on each girl's prom dress."

Growing up Rich
and Grounded

Yet alongside such indulgent (or negligent?) decisions are the choices of parents like Meg Whitman, who ran online auction behemoth eBay for a decade, before stepping down in March 2008. In 2007, *Forbes* estimated Whitman's worth at $1.4 billion. But as her net worth skyrocketed with the success of eBay, Whitman and her husband, Griffith Harsh, a neurosurgeon, made a conscious decision "not to change the way we live on a day-to-day basis." They wanted to emphasize their values for their two sons.

"Kids take their cues from their surroundings, including the house you live in, the car you drive, what you do together as a family," says Whitman. So through the years that their two sons attended high school and college, the couple drove a Grand Cherokee and a late-model hybrid. They chose not to trade up. "We live in a very nice, colonial-style house, but it's modest by Silicon Valley standards," says Whitman. Those parental decisions were validated not long ago, when her oldest son mentioned that staying in their house while he was in high school and not buying a bigger home made a "huge difference" for him, because he never felt uncomfortable among his friends.

There are other ways to communicate values to your kids, as well. In 2002, Whitman donated $30 million to build a new college at Princeton, which opened its doors in 2007. "Women give less money to their alma mater than men do," she says about the gift. "I wanted to change the averages."

Three Steps Toward Helping
Kids Develop the Habit
of Giving

Clearly enough, kids need a firm foundation for spending and saving before they can even contemplate giving. By helping them to define money's value and reach and to disconnect it from guilt or discomfort, you set the stage for the rewards and responsibilities of lifelong giving.

What follows is a three-part series of pointers from experienced advisors and affluent parents about how to instill a sense of identity, productivity, and, ultimately, compassion in kids. Many of these lessons overlap, of course. And you'll also need to evaluate the advice in light of each child's needs and stage of growth.

First, Teach the Value of a Buck

Start a routine of dividing your children's weekly or monthly allowance into three pots—for spending, saving, and giving. Very young kids can use jars to make this more tangible. This not only builds the habit of saving and giving but also helps develop money-management skills.

Follow the Warren Buffett example. When they're young, let your kids know they won't inherit much money, which will push them to make grown-up choices. "As someone who inherited, I really question the assumption that one should pass along a big inheritance," says philanthropist Marian Moore, who grew up in a wealthy family. "Kids have a better chance of creating their own lives and acting on their own vision and values without the burden of wealth."

Hold a family meeting and collaborate with your kids to draft a family compact or mission statement, with the idea that it will last for a few generations. Such meetings typically cover open discussions about the source of the family's money, how family members view their responsibilities about wealth, potential giving plans, and purposes or goals that can unite the family. The process helps everyone accommodate different opinions and visions. Set up regular times to review how family members are meeting the mission or goals you've established.

"If you don't manage the emotional and family aspects, the money doesn't matter," says Susan Remmer Ryzewic, who oversees the finances of the Remmer Family Foundation. For wealthy families, such meetings are becoming two- or three-day retreats that bring together extended branches of the family. "Wealth creates emotional hurdles, and I've had to deal with both my issues and my kid's issues," says Ryzewic, whose family came into its fortune when they sold her father's engineering business. "If you want to maintain the family legacy and not have it fall apart, it helps to uncover and figure out how to manage and resolve differences."

Second, Provide Relevant Lessons in Money Management

Spend time talking to your kids about the issues of values and financial education, teaching them the language of finances, and explaining how you research or review opportunities or big-ticket purchases. Do your children know how you arrive at major financial decisions?

Set up some kind of coaching sessions to tutor your kids in money management, whether on your own or with an outside advisor. Work with advisors who understand and talk about the emotional issues of money, not just the investment side of things. You can also start bringing the kids to meetings with your advisors from, say, age fourteen or so— including tax accountants or money and investment managers. That way they can learn about financial issues, see what it takes to assemble a good team of advisors, and become comfortable with the process of evaluating choices and making decisions on issues ranging from saving and investing to developing philanthropic plans and giving.

Giving Online Can Get Kids Started

Eyeing a burgeoning market opportunity, several online groups, both for-profit and nonprofit, are making it easier for kids to get involved in giving. Here are three popular options.

+ **ClubPenguin.com:** Owned by Disney, this is basically a Second Life–type virtual world for the youngster set. Club Penguin has both free- and paid-subscriber sections. For no charge, kids can create avatars and chat or play online games with peers around the world. Club membership (about $6 monthly) affords various perks, such as avatar costumes and entry into the "Global Citizenship" channel. Members can earn virtual coins by playing games; the coins and some of the membership fees are used for global charitable giving, including building schools, protecting the environment, and caring for needy children.

✦ **Kiva.org:** With a mission of leveraging individual micro-loans to ease worldwide poverty, founders Matt and Jessica Flannery launched this site in 2005. Lenders make loans of twenty-five dollars or more, via credit card. Kiva relays the money to a microfinance institution (MFI) in the borrower's home country, which pays out the funds and arranges repayment schedules. Kiva doesn't charge interest, but the MFIs do have low-level interest rates to cover costs and generate local income. To date, Kiva's 270,000 or so lenders have funded about 40,000 borrowers in forty countries, for a whopping $27 million in total funding. The charity has attracted some high-profile press, too. *New York Times* columnist Nicholas Kristof, for example, made a loan via Kiva and then traveled to Afghanistan to check out his borrowers—a baker and a TV repairman. Upon his return, Kristof wrote, "Web sites like Kiva are useful partly because they connect the donor directly to the beneficiary, without going through a bureaucratic and expensive layer of aid groups in between."

✦ **YouthGive.org:** Cofounders Jenny Yancey and Dan Siegel worked as advisors for charities before launching this nonprofit educational site. Based in northern California, YouthGive sets up modest donor-advised funds for each child contributor and his or her family. "Giving accounts" can be opened for as little as $1 or as much as $500. Donations go to nonprofits nominated or prescreened by the organization. Young donors post descriptions of their experiences and the groups on the site.

Third, Get the Kids Involved in Giving

Donors and parents who have been there and done it offer this advice.

Involve kids early. Youngsters can volunteer to gather food, clothing, or toys for needy groups.

Encourage your kids to save and donate money from their allowances. Work with your children to figure out how they want to donate the money set aside for giving.

Ask kids to help you research your own contributions, whether online, at a library, or over the phone.

Depending on the age of your children, require the real deal—research, site visits, financial reviews, conversations with the nonprofits' staff and grantees, and oversight for results and impact.

Create annual holiday rituals for community service or giving. It doesn't have to be complicated. The family can simply volunteer to help deliver food for Thanksgiving, host a fund-raising party for the local school or shelter, or collect clothing for the needy.

Let Kids Make Their Own Decisions

Many donors want their kids to participate in family-giving plans but take their interest for granted and won't give them any real authority. Try to avoid hovering, nagging, or putting strings on their choices. Let kids go about the process in their own way. If it seems a tad out of control, pull in a knowledgeable third party who can be objective. Keep listening. If you want the next generation to grow into the family's traditions and values, you must work at it.

For example, Shirley Fredericks, daughter of entertainer Lawrence Welk, ran the family's foundation for some seventeen years, actively supporting Los Angeles urban development. She turned over the reins to the next generation several years ago and now works with a group called YouthGive, based in Mill Valley, California.

"We created a junior board and brought on the 10 kids in 1983," says Fredericks. At the time, the youngest was fourteen and the oldest, twenty-four. "The junior board," she says, "was allowed to sit in on board meetings and vote 10 percent of the grant budget. But they had to do due diligence on the organizations they funded, including research and follow-up visits."

Increasingly, families are setting up discretionary funds for offspring, who may be scattered around the country, so the younger generation can support causes they choose in their own communities. And while parent-child tensions are inevitable as the lessons sink in, there are ways to defuse them.

A few years back, for instance, Ellen Remmer wanted her teenage kids—then fifteen and seventeen—to experience not simply the act of giving but the process of philanthropy. "I wanted them to learn about making a good grant, to learn how to give well, not necessarily to find the most important issue in the world to help."

She set up a meeting for the family with a facilitator at Boston's community foundation. Most of these public charities, as well as many private banks and financial services firms, will offer such help if you're a donor or client or if you might become one. The family's first hurdle in meeting with the facilitator was to reach a consensus about a category of giving that would engage them all—not a specific group or organization, mind you, but simply an area they all felt was worthy to fund. That took some weeks of discussion, with each family member assigned to researching and reporting back on specific subjects.

Through several meetings, everyone had a chance to talk about what was individually meaningful. Eventually, the family arrived at an area of interest that excited them all: services for new immigrants to Boston, along with programs that taught English as a second language. "We came together in our interest in education," says Remmer. "My son talked about groups that help people pull themselves up by their bootstraps, how to help people help themselves. My daughter wanted to focus on women in need. And my husband thought that funding immigrant education gave us the biggest bang for our buck."

The process had its ups and downs and dragged on as the teenagers moved in and out of focus, says Remmer. "I had to keep reminding myself that it was about developing a template for good giving, and not about giving together." After making several site visits, the family narrowed its choices down to two organizations,

STAGECRAFT

"Think of King Lear *as the story of a botched estate plan."*
—Phil Cubeta, GiftHub.org

with both teens arguing for their favorite. In the end, they compromised, giving each group $7,500.

What Does It Take to Fund a Legacy?

When thinking about the future and how to set up a legacy for yourself and the next generation, think big picture. Figure out what you own, what you want to accomplish, and what it will take to make that happen. Saving taxes isn't the goal. "You want to provide a legacy, not necessarily a financial inheritance," explains Melanie Schnoll-Begun, managing director for philanthropic services at Citigroup Global Wealth Management. "Tax implications should come second." A donor-advised fund can support a favored charity. Special endowments can bankroll foundations or causes. Trusts or investments can subsidize the dreams of loved ones and friends.

As you investigate the challenges of estate planning to form a charitable legacy, you also need to consider how to manage wealth for your heirs. "People who have worked hard for their wealth are very torn about how to pass it on," says Alyssa Moeder, a wealth advisor at Merrill Lynch's Private Banking & Investment Group. "The biggest question I get during estate planning is, 'What's the magic number? How much should I leave to the kids?'" Building on the foregoing advice on teaching kids about money, you may decide to rely on financial vehicles that hold the money in trust in some way so that the next generation is supported but doesn't have unlimited access.

A 529 college-savings program, for instance, can shelter money for qualified educational expenses. There are also health insurance trusts that can cover medical emergencies, and the widely known irrevocable trusts. Such arrangements can be structured to kick in over time, triggered by various life events or circumstances. "The issue of how much to give to the children, and when, is one of the many options to consider when setting up a trust," says Bill Barbeosch, chief fiduciary officer at GenSpring, a New York–based family wealth-management firm.

You will need advisors to steer you through the complicated scenarios. Each state has different estate laws and taxes. If you own property or businesses in more than one state, the process becomes multilayered. "People need long-term relationships with estate planning advisors that offer consistency and continuity," says trust advisor Patricia Angus. "Otherwise they end up with different documents by different people."

Keeping Family Philanthropy Alive and Well

As some of us are all too keenly aware, parents and children don't always think alike. And when it comes to passing on the values, mission, and financial control of a family's giving plan, things can get especially tricky.

Ashley Snowdon Blanchard, now in her early thirties, married, and a philanthropy consultant in New York at the

TCC Group, jumped those hurdles through steady perseverance.

Her great-grandfather Arthur Hill established the family's Hill-Snowdon Foundation in 1959. He had earned some money as an executive at Johnson & Johnson by choosing stock options in lieu of salary during World War II. Still, growing up in Washington, D.C., "we didn't really have that much money until my grandparents passed away," says Blanchard.

She remembers family members sitting around a kitchen table each year to decide where the foundation's grants would go. "Everyone had their own particular organizations and causes, and they'd all just give money to a school they attended, or the local animal shelter, because my aunt loved her cat. It wasn't thought out."

By 1997, when the foundation took charge of her grandparents' estates, "we had a rapid increase in assets," says Blanchard, who began attending foundation meetings as a teenager. "What had worked for people around the table didn't make sense for the next generation, and we brought a critical view to the status quo. There was an opportunity to put forth ideas without dipping into anyone's pot."

In the meantime, Blanchard had graduated from Stanford, studying nonprofit management and social-welfare policy. "I came of age when welfare reform was a hot-button social issue. The other huge issue was women's balancing act and the 'second shift' they worked at home. It was clearly a myth that women could do it all. I thought it was very unfair. If the upper middle class, my college friends, couldn't make it work, how could lower-income women? Ultimately, that led me to social change and philanthropy."

It was time for the forty-year-old foundation to grow up.

Within a few years, Blanchard had become president of the board, working to make the foundation strategic and focused on a consistent mission of social change and economic justice. The family also worked closely with a consultant from the Tides Foundation, a group based in San Francisco that counsels wealthy families and individuals about charitable plans. "We had a great working relationship," says Blanchard.

Nowadays, the Hill-Snowdon Foundation, with its endowment of roughly $37 million and annual grants of about $2 million, is pretty much on "cruise control and staff-driven." Blanchard works with the executive director to set agendas and keep the family informed and engaged. And she's begun to mentor the next generation, a young cousin who is a "trustee in training."

"We learn by doing," says Blanchard.

Chapter 11

WAYS AND MEANS

RESOURCES TO HELP YOU CREATE
A GIVING PLAN

ategorized by offerings and services, here are resources that can help you learn how to give more effectively and find organizations and experts. This listing reflects broad donor interests and education, sources for ongoing research into philanthropy, and independent organizations that offer a range of charitable options.

Advisors & Consultancies

21/64 (http://2164.net): A nonprofit division of the Andrea and Charles Bronfman Philanthropies that specializes in a multi-generational approach to giving.

International Association of Advisors in Philanthropy (advisorsinphilanthropy.org): Nonprofit professional membership organization for wealth managers and philanthropy advisors; offers a searchable directory.

The Philanthropic Initiative (tpi.org): Nonprofit that provides results-oriented philanthropy consulting to individuals, foundations, institutions, and corporations.

Rockefeller Philanthropy Advisors (rockapa.org): Helps donors, families, and foundations create and manage effective giving plans.

ResourceGeneration.org: Works with wealthy young people to effect social change through the strategic use of financial and other resources.

Tides Foundation (tidesfoundation.org): Provides philanthropic services and acts as an organizer and knowledge broker to support donors and nonprofits.

Blogs

TheAgitator.net: For fund-raisers and nonprofit executives and board members.

Beneblog.org: Focused on social good via technology; written by a rocket scientist turned social entrepreneur.

CharityFocus.org/blog: Focuses on how to get engaged and make a difference; written by a former software engineer who now runs a charity that provides free Web services to nonprofits.

Charity Governance Blog (charitygovernance.blogs.com): Written by a lawyer and accountant who delves into the stories behind the headlines of the philanthropy world.

DonorPowerBlog.com: Written by a fund-raising consultant who focuses on nonprofit-donor partnerships, to help charities appeal to boomer donors.

Don't Tell the Donor (donttellthedonor.blogspot.com): News and views from the world of nonprofit fund-raising.

FLiP (flip.typepad.com): Future Leaders in Philanthropy posts news and opinions from sector experts and consultants. Published by Changing Our World, a for-profit fund-raising consultancy.

GiftHub.org: Opinionated advice column for donors, written by a financial services executive.

Give & Take (philanthropy.com/giveandtake): A roundup of the charitable blogosphere from the *Chronicle of Philanthropy*.

SelfishGiving.org: A primer about cause marketing.

SocialEdge.org: Funded by the social entrepreneurial Skoll Foundation; offers blogs and discussion from many activists, including former president Jimmy Carter.

TacticalPhilanthropy.com: Written by a philanthropy consultant at an investment management firm; tracks trends in venture philanthropy.

Donor Education
& Best Practices

Center for Lobbying in the Public Interest (clpi.org): Promotes and supports nonprofit advocacy and lobbying to encourage civic participation.

Center on Philanthropy at Indiana University (philanthropy .iupui.edu): Provides research, academic programs, and degrees in nonprofit management, fund-raising, policy, and more.

Center for What Works (whatworks.org): Researches benchmarking for nonprofits to create frameworks and metrics for program outcomes and success.

Committee Encouraging Corporate Philanthropy (corpo ratephilanthropy.org): International forum of business CEOs and high-level executives focused on corporate philanthropy; the late actor Paul Newman was a cofounder.

Community Foundations of America (cfamerica.org): National association for the 700-plus community foundations around the country.

Emerging Practitioners in Philanthropy (epip.org): Works to educate and strengthen the next generation of grant makers.

FirstGov for Nonprofits (usa.gov/Business/Nonprofit.shtml): Network of links for federal government information and services.

Forum of Regional Association of Grantmakers (giving forum.org): National network of local leaders and grant makers that provides online information and resources for more effective giving.

GiveWell.net: Launched in 2008 by two young ex-hedge fund researchers, nonprofit that rates how effective charities are—unproven but creating buzz.

GrantCraft.org: Offers guides, videos, and case studies for the practitioner; a project of the Ford Foundation.

Grant Managers Network (gmnetwork.org): Provides a forum for information about grants management and effective grant making; affiliated with the Council on Foundations and the Rockefeller Family Fund.

Independent Sector (independentsector.org): A nonprofit membership coalition of charities and corporate-giving programs; lobbies on federal policy issues that affect charitable giving and offers online resources for the sector and donors.

National Committee on Planned Giving (ncpg.org): An association for professionals in the charitable-gift-planning field.

National Philanthropic Trust (nptrust.org): An independent public charity focused on developing philanthropic plans and solutions for donors.

Planned Giving Design Center (pdgc.com): Free resource (after registration) for in-depth news and advice about planned giving.

PNNOnline.org: A daily news and information service about nonprofits, with a focus on the United States.

RGK Center for Philanthropy and Community Service, University of Texas at Austin (utexas.edu/lbj/rgk): Academic programs, education, research, and community outreach.

Foundation Resources & Family Giving

Association of Small Foundations (smallfoundations.org): A membership organization that provides resources and networking for more than 3,000 foundations.

Council on Foundations (cof.org): A resource membership organization of 2,000 grant-making foundations and giving programs.

The Foundation Center (fdncenter.org): Advises more than 600 foundations and offers tools, research, and advice for grant givers and practitioners, including free e-newsletter "Philanthropy News Digest."

National Center for Family Philanthropy (ncfp.org): Educational resource for families and individuals that offers workshops, tools, and information for family grant makers.

Giving & Volunteering

Changemakers.net: A collaborative global online community that works on solutions for social change.

ChangingThePresent.org: Offers a range of different giving choices for individuals and families.

CharityFocus.org: Launched in 1999, an all-volunteer group that delivers free Web-related services to the nonprofit world.

Committee Encouraging Corporate Philanthropy (corporate philanthropy.org): Executive forum that hosts an online volunteer site that allows you to input your zip code and learn what's available in your area.

Corporation for National & Community Service (nationalservice.org): Established in 1993, an independent federal agency that engages millions of Americans in service through Senior Corps, AmeriCorps, Learn and Serve America, and other community programs.

Finca (villagebanking.org): The Foundation for International Community Assistance; began its international microfinance lending program in 1984.

GoodSearch.com: An Internet search engine powered by Yahoo! that raises money for charities by having advertisers pay a fee whenever users click on a given link.

Idealist.org: A project of Action Without Borders; site lists giving options for thousands of nonprofit and community organizations in nearly 200 countries.

The I Do Foundation (idofoundation.org): Created in 2002 by a group of nonprofit leaders and retailers; offers a charity registry for engagement or wedding gifts and allows people to donate a percentage of gifts to a selected charity.

The International Volunteer Programs Association (volunteer international.org): An alliance of nongovernmental organizations involved in international volunteer work and internship exchanges.

Network for Good (networkforgood.org): Founded in 2001 by America Online, Cisco Systems, and Yahoo! to combine resources for donors, volunteers, and organizations.

Points of Light Foundation (pointsoflight.org): After merging with Hands On Network in 2007, became one of the largest volunteer referral services in the nation.

Servenet.org: Launched in 1996 to connect youth volunteers with local nonprofits.

SixDegrees.org: Celebrity charitable network hosted by actor Kevin Bacon.

Social Venture Network (svn.org): A nonprofit member network of social entrepreneurs who share and leverage expertise and technology to find social solutions.

ThrowPlace.com: Site where companies and individuals around the world can post excess inventory or goods for donation; all items are given away.

USA Freedom Corps (volunteer.gov): Launched by President George W. Bush after September 11 as a federal initiative to encourage volunteer service.

VolunteerMatch.org: Helps you find a nearby and suitable volunteer opportunity from a list of 50,000 nonprofits.

Governance & Finances

BoardSource.org: An educational membership organization for nonprofit board members, senior staff, and consultants that offers workshops, online tools, training, and best practices for effective governance; about 12,000 members.

Free Management Library (managementhelp.org): A library for nonprofit and for-profit organizations, with an index of 675 topics.

IRS.gov (irs.gov/charities): Clear and in-depth resources about tax deductions, tax-exempt charities, and more.

National Council of Nonprofit Associations (ncna.org): Membership network of state and regional nonprofit associations that helps small and midsize nonprofits manage and lead more effectively.

Journals & E-newsletters

BlueAvocado.org: A twice-monthly free nonprofit e-magazine for community nonprofits.

The *Chronicle on Philanthropy* (philanthropy.com): The non-profit world's newspaper; published twice monthly.

The *Nonprofit Times* (nptimes.com): Focuses on nonprofit executive management.

Philanthropy Journal (philanthropyjournal.org): An educational Web site and free weekly newsletter for nonprofit news, resources, announcements, and job listings.

Kid-Friendly Sources

ClubPenguin.com: Virtual playdates for the youngster set, with an option to join the club for a fee and access the "Global Citizenship" channel; owned by Disney.

Kiva.org: Offers international microfinance giving options for kids and families.

LearningToGive.org: Educates kids about the importance of giving; free lessons and educational resources for teachers, parents, youth workers, faith groups, and community leaders.

Yes! Jams (yesjams.org): Global networking site for young people who want to make a difference.

YouthGive.org: Children and families set up modest "giving accounts" for a selection of evaluated charities.

Youth Service America (ysa.org): Established in 1986 to mobilize millions of youth for the annual National & Global Youth Service Day.

Research Groups

Aspen Institute (nonprofitresearch.org): Independent grantmaking organization for research into the nonprofit sector.

Center on Philanthropy and Public Policy at the University of Southern California (usc.edu/schools/sppd/philanthropy): Promotes and strengthens the nonprofit sector through research into philanthropy and public problem solving.

Center on Wealth and Philanthropy (bc.edu/research/cwp/): Research center at Boston College that studies spirituality, wealth, philanthropy, and cultural life.

GivingUSA.org: A leading philanthropy researcher; partners with the Center on Philanthropy at Indiana University to release a widely touted annual report about how much Americans give.

National Center for Charitable Statistics (nccs.orban.org): Clearinghouse of data on the nonprofit sector in the United States.

Nonprofit Academic Centers Council (nacouncil.org): Membership association of academic centers and programs at accredited colleges and universities that focus on the study of nonprofits, voluntarism, and/or philanthropy.

Special Interests

Asian Americans/Pacific Islanders in Philanthropy (aapip.org): National membership group of advocacy organizations to increase giving among Asian Pacific American communities.

Disability Funders Network (disabilityfunders.org): Works to increase the extent and effectiveness of grant making that benefits people with disabilities.

Hispanics in Philanthropy (hiponline.org): Promotes partnerships between organized philanthropy and Latino communities.

National Center for Black Philanthropy (ncfbp.net): Promotes and strengthens African American participation in philanthropy.

Native Americans in Philanthropy (nativephilanthropy.org): Engages Native and non-Native people in philanthropy that supports Native traditional values.

Women & Philanthropy (womenphil.org): A member network that works to increase dollars awarded to women and girls and the number of women working in the field.

The Twenty-first Century Foundation (21CF.org): Promotes African American participation and develops new models of black philanthropy to address issues in black communities.

Women's Funding Network (wfnet.org): Membership group of more than a hundred organizations that advance women's philanthropy and fund women's solutions around the world.

Tech Tools

501c3Cast.com: Podcasts for nonprofit pros and volunteers to share information and resources.

Blackbaud.com: One of the larger for-profit software and advisory companies that help organizations with fund-raising, donor acquisition, prospect research, performance benchmarking, and database services; there are a growing number of such services.

cMarket.com: Founded in 2002, this for-profit online bidding service generates funds for nonprofits by hosting virtual, on-demand charity auctions.

Donor Direct
(http://pcalc.ptec.com/hosts/hosts/demo/simpleMenu.html): Free planned-giving calculator for prospective donors who want to run scenarios about charitable deductions and giving vehicles.

Fidelity Charitable Services
(fidelitycharitableservices.com/charity-giving-help/tools.shtml): Several charitable- and estate-planning calculators and comparative-giving options.

Idealware.org: Provides candid reviews and articles about software of interest to nonprofits.

MobileActive.org: Supported by the Surdna Foundation, a New York–based family foundation, an all-volunteer social-network community for activists who are using mobile-technology communications to make a social impact.

NPower.org: A network of locally based nonprofit organizations that provide comprehensive and affordable technology assistance to other nonprofit groups.

NTEN.org: The Nonprofit Technology Network; a membership community of nonprofit pros who put technology to use for their causes.

Technology Affinity Group (tagtech.org): A public charity associated with the Council on Foundations; provides technology information, ideas, and tools for the foundation community.

TechSoup.org: Provides a range of technology services for nonprofits, including free articles, discussion forums, and discounted technology products.

Watchdogs

CharityNavigator.org: Rates large charities and organizations; about 5,000 groups in its database.

CharityWatch.org: A private group that rates charities by assigning a grade based on finances and spending; hosted by the American Institute of Philanthropy.

Federal Trade Commission (ftc.gov/charityfraud): Monitors and cracks down on charity fraud.

Give.org: The Better Business Bureau's Wise Giving Alliance; evaluates nonprofit organizations' standards; database of roughly 1,200 groups.

GuideStar.org: A searchable database with information on about 1.7 million tax-exempt nonprofits.

IRS (irs.gov): Offers searchable capability for its "Publication 78," a partial listing of about 695,000 qualified tax-exempt charities.

NASCO, National Association of State Charity Officials (nasconet.org): An association of state offices that oversee charities.

National Association of Attorneys General (naag.org): Offers database of state attorneys general whose offices typically monitor information and resources for nonprofits.

INDEX